with wings extended

with wings

A BUR OAK BOOK

holly carver,
series editor

extended

a leap into
the wood duck's
world

by greg hoch

university
of iowa press
iowa city

University of Iowa Press, Iowa City 52242
Copyright © 2020 by the University of Iowa Press
www.uipress.uiowa.edu
Printed in the United States of America

Design by Omega Clay

Printed on acid-free paper

Library of Congress Cataloging-in-Publication Data
Names: Hoch, Greg, 1971– author.
Title: With wings extended : a leap into the wood duck's world / by Greg Hoch.
Description: Iowa City : University of Iowa Press, [2020] | Series: Bur oak book | Includes bibliographical references and index.
Identifiers: LCCN 2019036761 (print) | LCCN 2019036762 (ebook) | ISBN 9781609386955 (paperback) | ISBN 9781609386962 (ebook)
Subjects: LCSH: Wood duck—North America. | Wood duck—North America—Conservation.
Classification: LCC QL696.A52 H595 2020 (print) | LCC QL696.A52 (ebook) |
DDC 598.4/123—dc23
LC record available at https://lccn.loc.gov/2019036761
LC ebook record available at https://lccn.loc.gov/2019036762

To Carrol, Tim, and Scott
Colleagues, Mentors, Friends

When at last she decides to bring out her young she makes a call or cluck that is difficult to describe. "Kuk, kuk, kuk" is repeated softly either from the nest entrance or a nearby limb or from the ground near the base of the tree. At once the ducklings can be heard peeping from the interior of the box. Very soon the first baby will appear at the hole, balancing there momentarily and sounding off with a staccato "pee, pee, pee, pee" repeated rapidly eight or ten times. Then, with tiny wings extended, the little fellow springs out to alight on the ground with a thump two or three feet from the base of the tree.—Frederic Leopold (1966)

contents

acknowledgments

First, I wish to thank Grant, Pat, and Paul for their leadership of the Division and Section. I also thank Bryan, Ricky, and Bob for daily guidance and friendship. I thank Commissioner Strommen, Barb, and Bob for their guidance from the top. I thank everyone on the west side of the second floor for your daily stimulating conversation, assistance when I need it, and camaraderie. (That means you too, Leslie.) Jim, I hope retirement is keeping your fishing line taut, and you're staying fit trying to keep up with grandkids. Tom and Dave, I hope the next chapters of your long careers are as fruitful as the past. Last, I thank all my colleagues outside the Central Office who do the day-to-day work to immediately benefit wildlife habitat.

I also want to thank all my friends and colleagues across Minnesota at the U.S. Fish and Wildlife Service. Ryan, Jean, and Becky, it still feels like coming home whenever I get a chance to visit. My thanks to Ducks Unlimited, Minnesota Waterfowl Association, Pheasants Forever, The Nature Conservancy, and everyone else who makes Minnesota a fun place to do conservation, both the big projects and the little details. We're much stronger working together than we would be working in isolation.

I thank the staff at the University of Iowa Press for their encouragement (and occasional goading), for their thoughtful comments and edits, and for helping me through the process of putting a book together, especially Holly, Meredith, and Susan.

Kevin, well, what else can I say. . . . Dave, we're at thirty years, and I'm still learning from you. John, as much as I learned from you in the office, I learned at least as much and probably more in the duck blind or over drinks after the hunt was over. I also thank Deanna for putting up with all the mud Ding and I track into the house.

preface

This is my third book on my third bird with the University of Iowa Press, members of the grouse, shorebird, and waterfowl families. They are very different birds. Greater prairie-chickens are relatively intolerant of trees in their habitat. Woodcock are dependent on young, or early successional, forest. Wood ducks, in contrast, rely on older trees with a diameter large enough to contain a cavity for them to nest in.

In each book, I've included direct quotations from early settlers, hunters, and researchers as well as more recent sources. Bellrose and Holm's *The Ecology and Management of the Wood Duck*, although a bit technical in some areas, is still the authoritative study on wood ducks. I've tried to emphasize in my three books how difficult it can be to manage habitat for each species and the size or scale of habitat we need to think about when managing for these species.

Taken together, these books show how any management we do, or don't do in many cases, will be beneficial to some species and detrimental to other species. For even a small parcel of habitat, say of forty acres or so, it can be challenging to manage for all of the dozens of species of wildlife people may be interested in.

This creates challenges for private landowners. If they can't manage everywhere for every species, they must decide what species or group of species they most want to encourage. For instance, it's easy to manage for both woodcock and golden-winged warblers. It may be more challenging, however, to manage for wood ducks and woodcock on the same small parcel.

We can add several levels of complexity for state and federal wildlife agencies, who need to manage numerous properties across a state or region both for a wide range of wildlife species and for all the needs of those species throughout the year. This can be especially challenging with migratory species, when management needs to be coordinated across state or international borders. Visualizing the landscapes a wood duck flies over during its migration from Minnesota to Louisiana shows how complicated this can be.

I have several goals with this book. First, I want to introduce or further inform readers about a duck they probably recognize but may not know well. Wood ducks have a number of characteristics that set them apart from other waterfowl species. Second, the book shows how almost anyone can get involved in conservation through nest boxes. Building and hanging a wood duck nest box allows people to do something for wildlife beyond writing checks to conservation organizations. Third, I hope to show the complexities of wildlife and habitat management that landowners as well as state and federal wildlife agencies deal with on a daily basis.

The story of the wood duck is an amazing conservation story. A century ago, many people had given up on the wood duck, fearing it was doomed to extinction along with the passenger pigeon and Carolina parakeet. Today, it's one of the most familiar and most harvested ducks in the eastern half of the country. The wood duck is one of America's great conservation stories.

with wings extended

introduction   a most beautiful duck

> What an ornament to a river to see that glowing gem floating in contact with its waters! As if the hummingbird should recline its ruby throat and its breast upon the water. Like dipping a glowing coal in water! It so affected me.—*Thoreau 1855*
>
> If the end of a rainbow had touched a marsh and dabbled its colors over a plain brown duck, it could never produce anything half so brilliant as one of these old male wood ducks in full breeding plumage.—*Bailey 1902*
>
> Few if any more exquisitely beautiful creatures have been fashioned in the workshop of nature than the Wood Ducks of America.—*Dawson 1903*
>
> The dog whines and I see the wood duck drake. I wouldn't have seen it until too late if she hadn't alerted me. She brings the bird back and I hold it. It's like cupping a sunset. —*Hill 1987*

This is the most beautiful duck on earth.

This opening sentence pays homage to a duck and a literary master-piece. At least thirty descriptions of the wood duck in the ornithology and waterfowl literature have the words "most beautiful" in the first sentence. This sentence also pays tribute to the introduction to one of the classics of American environmental or conservation literature and my personal favorite first line of any book. Unfortunately for our purposes here, Edward Abbey's *Desert Solitaire* isn't related to waterfowl at all. But it's still a darn good way to start a book.

Alexander Wilson and John Audubon, the fathers and founders of American ornithology, started this "most beautiful" trend in the early 1800s. In addition to being beautiful, the wood duck is one of the most unusual birds in North America. It's the original odd duck.

While most ducks nest on the ground, the wood duck is one of the few ducks that nest in tree cavities. The other North American cavity nesters are mergansers, buffleheads, and goldeneyes. Wood ducks, *Aix sponsa*, are also one of only four North American ducks that taxonomists list as the sole members of their genus, the others being the Steller's eider, harlequin duck, and long-tailed duck. Woodies are one of only two species that share the genus *Aix*, the other being the mandarin duck of China.

Wood ducks are as comfortable perching on tree limbs as they are paddling around wetlands. This ability to perch on tree limbs opens up food resources that few other ducks have.

> [W]oodies fly into trees where grapevines are twined and snatch the grapes from the arboreal perches. (Bellrose 1976)

Most ducks nest in the prairie pothole region in the northern Great Plains, the northern tundra, or the boreal forest. Wood ducks nest across eastern North America, as far south as Florida and Texas. A second population lives in the Pacific Northwest.

Adjectives for wood duck habitat include solitary, small, dark, still, secluded, quiet, pools, backwaters. But wood ducks are also known for nesting near people.

> This fowl delights in the small streams and mill-ponds of the interior, and is but seldom met with on the large rivers. (Lewis 1906)

> These ducks often built their nests in the hollow trees of the orchard or in the shade tree that overhung the farmhouse. (Forbush 1925)

People have been able to use this information to both benefit the ducks and entertain themselves by mounting nest boxes. Wood duck enthusiasts can watch the hen come and go each day, and if they are lucky, watch ten or twelve fluffy balls with splayed out webbed feet descend gently to the ground one morning.

> "Here they come," I whispered to the people huddled on our balcony. All froze. A male and female wood duck flew full speed toward the wood duck box. (Bradley 1985)

With webbed feet and downy wings outstretched, the duckling plummets downward to splash on the water or bounce like a ball on the ground. (Hester and Dermid 1973)

In the late 1800s and early 1900s, wood ducks became so rare in many parts of their range that they were once given up as destined for extinction. In fact, there was so much concern about wood ducks in the early twentieth century that they were one of the few birds specifically identified in the Migratory Bird Treaty of 1916.

Article IV. The High Contracting Powers agree that special protection shall be given the wood duck and the eider duck either (1) by a close season extending over a period of at least five years, or (2) by the establishment of refuges, or (3) by such other regulations as may be deemed appropriate.

Although not generally encouraged among most conservationists today, wood ducks have been kept in captivity and can be tamed. Phillips (1925) states that rearing wood ducks in captivity is such a fascinating subject that an entire book could be written on that topic alone.

The Wood-duck is frequently domesticated in Canada and is very easily tamed. (King 1866)

The wood duck is often kept in confinement, and it is a beautiful pet. (Grinnell 1901)

There are records of wood ducks in England as early as 1747 and as being part of an aviary in France as early as 1663 (Phillips 1925). Eventually some ducks were even shipped back to the United States.

At that time [early twentieth century] there were said to be more Wood Ducks in Belgium than in the United States. (Forbush 1925)

Also, Holland is rearing a lot of American Wood ducks and selling them back to us for big prices. (Bendick 1931)

In recent years, they have been the most harvested duck in the Atlantic Flyway, topping even the ubiquitous and abundant mallard. They are always near the top of the most harvested duck list in the Mississippi Flyway. From near extinction to most harvested bird is quite the conservation success story.

Wood ducks have faced a number of threats, some in common with other waterfowl, others somewhat exclusive to this species. In common, wood ducks face the same threats to wetland number and wetland quality that all ducks face. Wetlands are drained, streams are straightened, rivers are diked and channelized, and waters almost everywhere in the Midwest are polluted with sediment and chemical run-off from agricultural fields.

A few issues affect wood ducks that most other waterfowl don't have to deal with, however. The first is the cutting of forests across eastern North America in the late 1700s and 1800s. Wood ducks are dependent on old trees large enough to have hollow cavities for them to nest in. During the Timber Baron days, large, old, hollow trees were few and far between.

Many of those hollow cavities were made by woodpeckers, especially pileated and ivory-billed woodpeckers. The loss of large trees and hunting damaged their populations also. The ivory-billed has probably been driven to extinction. Together, the loss of trees and woodpeckers has meant fewer trees and fewer cavities for wood ducks. In addition, wood ducks are especially fond of beaver ponds. By the mid-to-late 1800s, however, beavers were trapped to local extinction across much of the eastern United States.

I found a pair near Henderson, in Kentucky, with eggs in the beginning of April, in the abandoned nest of an ivory-billed woodpecker. (Audubon 1840)

A large beaver pond is usually ideal wood duck habitat and is especially suited to rearing young. We have often thought that the beaver is the best friend a wood duck ever had. (Hester and Dermid 1973)

The loss of old growth forests, woodpeckers, and beavers at essentially the same period in our country's history was devastating to wood ducks.

Another name for the wood duck was the summer duck. In the 1700s and early 1800s, most Americans, at least those of European descent, were confined to the eastern part of the continent. Ducks were phenomena of spring and fall for those at mid-to-northern latitudes. For those in the South, waterfowl were commonly seen only in the winter months. In the summer people just didn't see ducks, except . . . . Because of their unusual nesting habitat, species range, and migratory patterns, wood ducks were a common sight any time of the year. They were especially conspicuous during the summer, when they were the only ducks around.

> When March has again returned, and the Dogwood expands its pure blossoms in the sun, the Cranes soar away on their broad wings, bidding our country adieu for a season, flocks of water-fowl are pursuing their early migrations, the frogs issue from their muddy beds to pipe a few notes of languid joy, the Swallow has just arrived, and the Blue-bird has returned to his box. The Wood Duck almost alone remains on the pool.
> (Audubon 1840)

Their persistence in summer was another large part of the wood duck's brush with extinction. Today, it's only legal to hunt most migratory birds in the fall, after the breeding season, as young and old alike head south to their wintering habitats. Before the Migratory Bird Treaty (1916) and Migratory Bird Treaty Act (1918), waterfowl were hunted spring and fall, and in the case of the wood duck, virtually year-round in many regions.

By the time most ducks arrived on their nesting grounds in the Great Plains or Prairie Provinces, they had left the hunters behind them. They could nest and raise young relatively unmolested. Wood ducks were always under the gun.

> Living as it does, throughout its range, close to human habitation, it has been an easy mark for every type of shooter, from the farm lad up.
> (Kortright 1943)

The scientific name of the wood duck is *Aix sponsa*. According to Kortright (1943) *Aix* is Greek for "a kind of waterfowl in Aristotle," while *sponsa* is Latin for "betrothed, i.e., as if in wedding dress, referring to the beautiful." Of course, in wood ducks and most waterfowl, it's the male (groom) and not the female (bride) that is brightly colored.

Today, wood ducks are one of the most popular ducks for bird hunters and bird watchers. That has made them a popular subject for artists to paint, taxidermists to mount, or carvers to make as working or decorative decoys. Wood ducks can drive artists a little crazy though.

> Probably no avian specimen has frustrated carvers more than the wood duck drake. (Frank 1982)

The drake and hen wood duck. The woody was often referred to as the bridal duck, although like most birds the male is more highly ornamented.
Photo courtesy of Carrol Henderson.

Wood ducks are a bit tricky to paint, because it's easy to overdo their colors. (Maass 1990)

Don't try to show all sides of a Wood Duck, even though you know it's beautiful all the way around. (Jackson 2007)

Wood ducks have appeared on the Federal Duck Stamp four times: in 1943 painted by Walter Bohl, in 1974 by David Maass, in 2012 by Joe Hautman, and in 2019 by Scot Storm. The wood duck has also been on numerous state waterfowl stamps. Wood ducks have not had a lot of attention from writers over the years, however.

Thus, the striking feature of the early history of modern knowledge of the wood duck is the paucity of writings despite the bird's widespread distribution. (Reeves 1988)

We can speculate on reasons for this. First, in the 1800s, during the market hunting days, hunters were after the maximum harvest each day. That meant big flights of big ducks on big waters. Sitting on a quiet little stream hoping a couple woodies fly by wouldn't pay the bills. Some records show wood ducks for sale in markets from New York to New Orleans. But they were probably never as popular with hunters as mallards or the diving ducks, such as canvasbacks and scaup. Second, much was written about sport hunting of waterfowl in the 1920s and 1930s. From 1918 to 1941, literally between the wars, the wood duck season was closed.

Dozens of researchers, conservationists, bird hunters, and birdwatchers have dedicated significant portions of their lives to waterfowl generally and to wood ducks specifically, but four names are really most associated with wood ducks. Three had long, distinguished, and diverse careers not limited to any one species, but we have to assume that these little ducks held a special place in each of their hearts.

Frank Bellrose started with the Illinois Natural History Survey in 1938. He helped pioneer aerial waterfowl surveys, and his research was instrumental in banning lead shot for waterfowl hunting. In 1976, he revised Kortright's *Ducks, Geese, and Swans of North America*, a major undertaking. The Waterfowl Research Laboratory in Illinois was named for him in 1997. His obituary in the journal *The Auk* (Fredrickson and Havera 2005) stated that an eminent waterfowl expert was asked to name the three leading waterfowl experts. The answer: "Frank Bellrose, and I don't know the other two." His obituary also stated that "early on, the name Bellrose became synonymous with the Wood Duck." Bellrose cowrote *The Ecology and Management of the Wood Duck*.

In 1940, Art Hawkins and Frank Bellrose published "Wood Duck Habitat Management in Illinois." Art Hawkins was one of Aldo Leopold's graduate students, their professional relationship starting at 8:30 a.m. on January 2, 1935 (Hawkins 1988). Three years later, Hawkins moved to Illinois, where he worked with Frank Bellrose before being called away to World War II.

In *Aldo Leopold: Mentor* (1988), Hawkins recalls how he hadn't finished publishing his graduate research before leaving to take his first job in Illinois. This is a perennial issue for many graduate students still today. He recounts receiving a letter from Professor Leopold in May 1938 asking him how the manuscript was coming. In one of the great Freudian slips in wildlife history, Hawkins (1940) lists the mammals of Faville Grove, Wisconsin, as "bear, raccoon, buffalo, moose, deer, fox squirrel, wood duck, rabbit (several varieties), and wolf." Presumably he meant wood chuck! That typo, however, foreshadowed a long and distinguished career.

Aldo Leopold asked Art to stop by and introduce himself to the Leopold family across the Mississippi in Burlington, Iowa. Art hit it off especially well with Frederic Leopold, Aldo's youngest brother. While not a professional biologist, Frederic's life is a testament to the impact one person can have. He started a nest-box program in his yard. When Frederic passed away in 1989, his boxes had produced more than 5,000 ducklings (Hawkins 1994).

After returning from the war, Art took a position with the U.S. Fish and Wildlife Service. Art helped develop the Flyway Council System and helped organize the Mississippi Flyway Waterfowl Committee. He is described as a "pioneer in waterfowl management" and a "legend within the migratory bird fraternity" (Nelson et al. 2007). In 1985, Art Hawkins helped form the Wood Duck Society. Another founding member of that society was Walter Breckenridge.

Breckenridge started as a preparator and spent the last twenty-four years of his career as the director of the James Ford Bell Museum of Natural History at the University of Minnesota. Breckenridge was a writer, painter, and filmmaker. He gave hundreds of lectures on conservation over his career. All of these efforts focused on bird conservation. In 1995, the University of Minnesota established the Breckenridge Chair of Ornithology (Tordoff 2004). Luce (2003) stated that wood ducks may have been Breckenridge's favorite duck. That statement is borne out by the number of wood duck drawings and paintings he produced. The front cover of his autobiography features a pair of woodies.

In the field of waterfowl conservation, and wildlife conservation in general, one name rises above all: Frederic's oldest brother, Aldo Leopold. Hawkins (1994) states that he never saw Leopold climb a tree to check a nest box, harvest a wood duck, or touch a wood duck museum specimen. He also wrote that there are few mentions of wood ducks in Leopold's writings (to the frustration of the author of this book). Because of the impacts Leopold had on conservation philosophy, policy, and implementation, however, Hawkins continues by writing:

> Aldo Leopold's indirect hidden-hand had more far-reaching efforts on wood ducks than any of us hands-on wood-duckers could hope to achieve. (Hawkins 1994)

1 taxonomy and anatomy

It is called the Wood Duck, from the circumstance of its breeding in hollow trees; and the Summer Duck, from remaining with us chiefly during the summer.—*Wilson 1839*

The Wood Duck is conspicuous for the swiftness, ease, and elegance of its flight. It can pass through woods, and among the branches of the trees, with as much facility as the Wild Pigeon.—*Baird et al. 1884*

It is also often known as the Bridal Duck, although Summer Duck is more frequently applied.—*Reed 1912*

The Carolina Duck is an inhabitant of deciduous forests and small inland waterways. —*Phillips 1925*

What are the characteristics that differentiate waterfowl from other types of birds? What other birds are waterfowl most closely related to? Among the waterfowl, what are the primary ways to determine if a species belongs with the swans or geese or belongs with the ducks? Among the ducks, how do we determine if a species should be placed with the dabbling or puddle ducks, diving ducks and sea ducks, perching ducks, stiff-tailed ducks, or mergansers? Should perching ducks be separated out, or should they be combined with dabbling ducks?

As with many species, wood ducks have had a number of common names over the years and in different parts of the country. Phillips (1925) lists thirteen different names in English, seven in French, and five in German. Kortright (1943) lists sixteen common names in different regions of the United States. In addition to wood duck, some of the most common names for this species are summer duck (where they nest), acorn duck (what they eat), or squealers (what they sound like). Of course, many people just call them woodies.

Every high school biology student learns about taxonomy by studying the Linnaean system for organizing all life: kingdom, phylum, class, order, family, genus, and species. Scientists use the genus and species classifications to label a species, transforming "wood duck" into *Aix sponsa*. As scientists identify more and more species, some of these categories have been subdivided. A family can contain multiple subfamilies, and subfamilies can be split into tribes. Agreement isn't perfect, however, on how these further groups and species should be arranged. Taxonomists often develop evolutionary trees to show relationships between different species and groups of species. One of their most challenging tasks is determining which characteristics are of primary and which are of secondary importance in determining the branches or forks in these trees. Characteristics considered can include "studies of structure, plumage, physiology, habits, and courtship behavior" (Bellrose 1976). In more recent decades we can add genetics.

The decisions often get harder the higher up in the tree we get. Clearly a duck is different from a sparrow, warbler, hawk, or owl. It's easy to see that a mallard is a duck and a Canada goose is a goose. But look at a green-winged teal, a blue-winged teal, a northern shoveler, and a gadwall. Which two are most closely related? Which species is most closely related to those two? How are those decisions made, and what characteristics are those decisions based on? Taxonomists ask lots of challenging questions and must make lots of difficult decisions.

In the first edition of *Ducks, Geese, and Swans of North America*, Kortright (1943) places wood ducks in the subfamily Anatinae, river and pond ducks or surface-feeding ducks. A later edition of the same book, written by Bellrose (1976), divides the subfamily Anatinae into tribes and places wood ducks in the tribe Carinini. In the latest edition of the same book, now written by Baldassarre (2014), wood ducks are placed in the tribe Anatini with the puddle or surface-feeding ducks.

Delacour and Mayr (1945) were the first to place wood ducks in the tribe Carinini or Cairinini, perching ducks. They described the perching duck tribe as "very peculiar groups of ducks." Johnsgard (1968), who also placed them in the same tribe, introduces the perching ducks by stating that "this group of thirteen species [worldwide] is a rather heterogeneous assemblage that is not easily characterized." The perching duck tribe and the wood duck have obviously caused some confusion over the years. Phillips (1925) states that taxonomists changed the wood duck's scientific name and classification nine times between 1758 and 1883. It has obviously changed a few times since then. Delineating the relationship of perching ducks to other ducks is also challenging. Obviously many taxonomists simply combine wood ducks with dabbling ducks, implying that they are closely related. Johnsgard (2010) states that Delacour and Mayr, according to their 1945 descriptions, "believed the nearest relatives of the perching ducks to be the sea ducks, but I pointed out . . . the perching ducks' nearest relatives are the dabbling ducks." In 1968, Johnsgard wrote "the two tribes are obviously closely related, and taxonomists are not agreed on which group some species . . . should be included in."

Livezey (1986) describes woodies as belonging to a "a poorly resolved grade of 'perching' and 'dabbling' genera." He goes on to state that the tribe Carinini "has been recognized by subsequent workers in spite of the equivocal allocation of several genera, the widely recognized heterogeneity of its members in behavior, morphology, and biochemistry . . . and the conspicuous lack of a single character or combination of characters that uniquely distinguishes its members from other anatines." Delacour and Mayr (1945) further muddy the water by stating that wood ducks are one of three species that "seem to bridge the gap between the river ducks and the perching ducks." Put another way, this may be a bit of a catch-all group. If a species doesn't clearly fit somewhere else, this is one possible place to put them.

Genetics should help. Nothing is more basic than looking at an individual's or a species' DNA. Even the genetic data can vary, depending on what test the geneticists conduct and what genetic markers they use. Oates and Principato (1994) state that "*Aix* is closest to *Anas* on the distance Wagner diagram, but closest to *Aythya* on the phenogram." In other words, sometimes wood ducks (*Aix*) appear to be more closely related to dabbling ducks (genus *Anas*) and sometimes they appear to be more closely related to diving ducks (genus *Aythya*).

What does all of this mean? Here are two take-aways. First, the relationship of one species to another, and even of one group to another, is far, far more complicated than high school and college textbooks depict. Second, these relationships and the confusion they can generate demonstrate how dynamic the natural world is. Delacour and Mayr (1945) state that "there are a number of species and genera that are either intermediate between the otherwise well-defined tribes or too poorly known for a safe classification; others show peculiarities or a combination of characters that prevent them from fitting well into any existing group." Evolution is actively going on around us.

G. Evelyn Hutchinson, one of the world's most famous ecologists, is widely known for expressing the concept of "ecological theater and evolutionary play." By this he meant that a habitat or environment provides the location—the theater—in which evolution—the play—unfolds. The evolution of a species takes place within the context of the species' ecology. Ecological pressures cause the species to evolve.

A species' anatomy provides one of the clearest views of its evolution. Most ducks inhabit prairies or tundras, wide-open spaces. They need to be able to fly fast in a straight line. They don't need to twist or turn, zig or zag. When you live in the prairie nothing gets in the way of your flight. Wood ducks live among trees. As such, they do need to be able to twist and turn among the branches. After their feathers, this is one of the most written about features of the wood duck.

> The flight of the wood duck is swift and graceful, and the bird rivals the grouse and quail in the ease and facility with which it glides through the woods and among the branches. (Fisher 1901)

> It is as much at home in the woods as a Grouse and finds its way among the trees with perfect ease when flying at full speed, and is frequently seen perched on trees and stumps. (Eaton 1910)

In flight the Wood Duck is swift and direct when in the open, but it can penetrate among the many branches of the woods as swiftly and surely as a Ruffed Grouse or Passenger Pigeon, twisting and turning rapidly in avoiding the many obstacles in its way. (Forbush 1912)

Besides being the acknowledged leader in beauty, the Wood Duck rates as the most expert of fliers, threading his way as surely and as swiftly among the tree tops as the carrier [passenger] pigeon. (Bruette 1930)

One reason wood ducks are able to zig and zag like this is because they have a much larger tail than most ducks, which acts something like a rudder. Indeed, with a few other exceptions, such as the pintail and the long-tailed duck, most waterfowl have hardly any tail at all. The pintail's tail is mostly for show, but the wood duck's tail is quite utilitarian.

One distinguishing feature of a wood duck in the air is the square-shaped tail. His flight is fast; he has a high ratio of wing area to body weight and his relatively large tail makes for quick, sharp turns so necessary for flying among trees. (McQueeny 1946)

The wood duck's wings are also slightly modified to facilitate maneuvering through tree limbs. Bellrose and Holm (1994) cite their unpublished data showing that wood ducks have the broadest wing relative to length of any duck. Long, narrow, pointed wings are ideal for straight, fast flight. Shorter, stubbier, more rounded wings, like those of quail and ruffed grouse, are good for zigging and zagging, but not for long, sustained flight. Members of the grouse family aren't migratory. Even if they wanted to escape the winter, they simply don't have the wings for it.

Wood duck wings are a compromise, and compromising is what evolution does best. If wood ducks only needed to migrate long distances, they would have longer, narrower wings. If wood ducks only had to fly through the trees, they would have the short, rounded wings of grouse or forest songbirds. Because they need to be able to do both, however, their anatomy is a compromise. They still have the more pointed wing tips of the fast fliers

The long tail of the wood duck compared to the short, stubby tail of a dabbling duck like the northern shoveler. *Photos courtesy of Carrol Henderson.*

of open country, but their wings are a little broader than others, more similar to those of forested species that need to weave through the branches. Compromise.

Ducks are well known for their comic waddling walk. In fact, the legs of diving ducks are set so far back on the body that they are extremely awkward when walking on land and rarely leave the water. Dabbling or puddle ducks also have legs set relatively far back on their bodies. This makes it easy for both diving and dabbling ducks to tuck their feet up beneath them when flying, to reduce drag. It also makes it easier to paddle. For diving ducks, having legs far back on the body makes it easier for them to propel themselves under water. Think of the screws located on the back end of a submarine. Wood duck legs are set just a little farther forward on their bodies. This allows them to be more balanced and to walk a little more gracefully on land.

> [I]t wanders far out into the drier parts of the woods to pick up acorns, nuts, grapes, and berries, and the seeds of various trees and shrubs.
> (Mabbott 1920)

More importantly, wood ducks need to land and balance on tree limbs. And then they walk along that limb. Walking along a limb is fine. Waddling along a limb doesn't seem as steady or safe. This ability allows them to exploit a food source not available to most other ducks.

> They perch readily upon the branches of trees, and even walk along them without hesitancy. (Dawson 1903)

After the feathers and the tail, a third highly noticeable feature of wood ducks is their large eye. Bellrose and Holm (1994) write that wood ducks have the largest eyes of any North American duck relative to body weight. Larger eyes gather more light, which is useful in the low light and shadowy conditions of forests at dawn and dusk. Many ducks and geese fly in low light conditions as well, however. Bellrose and Holm speculate that the wood duck's larger eye allows it to pick out details that other ducks might miss—a critical skill when flying through a forest's maze of branches.

Wood ducks, and really all species, take form through a set of evolutionary compromises, which can often make it difficult to determine the specific branch in the tree of life they should perch on. Considering these compromises shows how dynamic the natural world is. Evolution isn't something that can be learned from history books. Evolution is something to learn in current events classes. As Delacour and Mayr (1945) state, "many genera . . . present convincing evidence of active speciation."

2 endless forms most beautiful

Peerless amongst its entire family for its indescribable beauty stands the Wood Duck
. . . . It is at once the Prince of Ducks. The most truthful and esthetic descriptions of the
mature male could reach no nearer the limning reality than the coldest prose could paint
the rainbow. Science, after all her most imposing assumptions, would sit down and weep
before the task, in blank despair.—*Hatch 1892*

That duck was all jewels combined, showing different lusters as it turned on the unrippled
element in various lights, now brilliant glossy green, now dusky violet, now a rich bronze,
now the reflections that sleep in the ruby's grain.—*Thoreau 1855*

Literally all the colors of the rainbow belong to this bird in his nuptial plumage, with black
and white thrown in for good measure.—*Dawson 1903*

Two different times I saw him riding the water dressed as the Shah of Persia.—*Porter 1919*

The last sentence of the previous chapter evokes one of the most famous and often quoted lines in all of biology, the final sentence of Charles Darwin's *On the Origin of Species* (1859): "from so simple a beginning endless forms most beautiful and most wonderful have been, and are being, evolved." Darwin wasn't talking about the beauty of a single species, but about the beauty of the process of evolution. With little question, some of the most beautiful animals in the world are birds. And, of course, it is feathers that make them beautiful.

Feathers keep birds warm on cold days, especially the fluffy, downy feathers close to the bird's body. Anyone who has worn a down jacket is familiar with the insulating properties of feathers. In other cases, feathers may help birds in hot and/or sunny climates keep cool. In fact, it may be better to say that feathers help regulate body temperature. Feathers also aid birds, especially the males in some species, in advertising their virility.

Lastly, in the evolution of function, feathers, especially the long feathers on the backside of the wing and the tail, aid in flying.

Where did feathers come from? Or, put another way, which came first, the chicken (or duck) or the egg? The egg. What laid the egg? A dinosaur or, more specifically, a theropod dinosaur. *Tyrannosaurus rex* is an example of a theropod.

That's an oversimplification, but scientists are pretty sure that modern birds are direct descendants of ancient dinosaurs. In fact, many of the dinosaurs originally thought to have been covered with reptilian scales were probably also covered with feathers. These early feathers would have not been large enough to help the creature fly, but they could have provided insulation. Researchers have shown that many dinosaur feathers were brightly colored and formed sometimes complex patterns on the dinosaurs' bodies, indicating that they may have played a role in advertising the males' sexual fitness. The evolution of flight is an entire field of its own, but generally we can say that feathers evolved first for insulation and sexual advertising; only later did the long wing and tail feathers helpful for flight evolve.

The first thing anyone notices about wood ducks are the bold colors of the male. And there are so many colors. This brings up the twin questions of how and why the feathers are so colorful. Explaining the "how" is suitable for the physics classroom; "why" is more of a biological question. Among the ducks, redheads do have red heads, but green-headed mallards don't have green heads, and blue-winged teal don't have blue wings. The feathers only look green-blue.

Feather color has two sources: some colors are pigment-based and others are structural. Yellow, red, brown, black, and white feathers are colored by pigments in the feather. Blues and greens result from microscopic surface features of the feathers. One of the analogies most often used to describe this phenomenon is the soap bubble. When looking at a soap bubble the eye sees shimmering blues, greens, reds, oranges, purples, and so on. But the bubble isn't actually any of those colors. The feathers on the head of a mallard, wood duck, shoveler, bufflehead, and other ducks show that

The bold iridescent colors on the head and back of the wood duck drake have a different origin than the reds and yellows on the chest and flank.
Photo courtesy of Carrol Henderson.

same rainbow of color for similar reasons. Examine a mallard's or wood duck's green head in bright light or in a color photograph. Overall, the head looks green, but iridescent blues, purples, and other colors are present as well. Other areas will look black. If the observer moves around the bird or the bird turns, those colors seem to shimmer and shift.

> Hues change constantly with changes in light refraction, adding still greater variety to the many iridescent colors. (Bellrose 1976)

Likewise, in low light, many of those blues and greens disappear. In *Deep Enough for Ivorybills* (1988), James Kilgo describes holding a wood duck drake he had just harvested in the half-light of sunrise, stating "I admired the crested black head." He didn't say the head was green because in the early morning there was not enough light to make the feathers look iridescent.

We can see this in another way: grind up a red feather from a cardinal or a yellow feather from a goldfinch. The result will be a small pile of red to yellow dust, because those colors are pigments within the feather. Grind up a blue or green feather, and the dust will be black, because those colors in the feathers result from surface structures reflecting light back to the eye. Those structures are destroyed when ground up. Another way to see this phenomenon is by looking at both sides of a feather. A brown, yellow, or red feather looks brown, yellow, or red on both sides. If you look at a green or blue feather, the side facing out will have color, while the side facing the bird's body will generally look black.

In many feathers, the beauty emerges from the interaction of pigment and structural colors, resulting in the wide range of colors we see in bird feathers. Humans, however, are limited in what colors they can see, relative to the vision of many bird species that can see into the ultraviolet spectrum. Imagine walking around all the time under a black light. The effect might approach how some birds see other birds and the rest of the world. Drab sparrows may actually be quite colorful in the eyes of other sparrows.

Descriptions of the wood duck's plumage are often much longer than similar descriptions for other birds. Writers often resort to creative uses of the color spectrum. Goss (1891) used the following in his descriptions of the drake wood duck: "silky metallic green, violet, and purple . . . soft violaceous black . . . dark metallic green . . . metallic reddish purple . . . rich purple chestnut . . . pale fulvous buff, delicately undulated with black . . . rusty fulvous . . . dark slaty brownish, very faintly glossed with bronze . . . bronze green reflections . . . rich dark metallic maroon purple . . . rich velvety reflections of blue, green, and purple . . . greenish bronze color . . . purplish steel blue."

Below are quotes from two scientists, followed by quotes from two artists. These different observers, with different perspectives, all share a common theme regarding color and iridescence.

A line from the bill over the eye, a similar line at the base of the side of the crest, and some of the elongated crest feathers white; throat, a band from it up the side of the head, and a wider one to the nape, white; rest of the cheeks and crown green with purplish reflections; a white band in front of the wings; breast and a spot at either side of the base of the tail purplish chestnut, the former spotted with white; belly white; sides buffy ochraceous, finely barred with black, the longer flank feathers tipped with wider bars of black and white; back greenish brown, scapulars black; speculum steel-blue; primaries tipped with greenish-blue. (Chapman 1907)

. . . remainder of the head silky metallic green, violet, and purple, as follows: cheeks and space behind the white cheek-bar soft violaceous-black, in the latter region extending up to the lower white stripe, but in the anterior region bounded above and anteriorly by dark metallic green; the orbital region and anterior half of the crest between the white lines metallic reddish-purple; forehead, crown, and posterior portion of the crest metallic green; terminal portion of the crest, above, laterally, and beneath, dark metallic violet. . . . Back, lesser wing-coverts, and rump dark slaty brownish, very faintly glossed with bronze, the wing coverts more slaty, the rump much darker, and gradually deepening into black toward the upper tail coverts, which with the tail, or deep black, the latter with bronze-green reflections in certain lights. . . . Tertials and posterior scapulars intense black, with rich velvety reflections of blue, green, and purple (chiefly the first) in certain lights. . . . (Ridgway 1913)

The portrayal of iridescence demanded a kind of sacrifice. I could not put down all the lovely color that I knew was there. I had to be content with what I could see from one angle, and that angle only. (Sutton 1979)

How would I find those depths of burgundy or make the iridescence of its scapulars and speculum? At the base of the tail on either side there was a spray of color I'd never seen in any palette. . . . I turned it over in my hand and caught the small flash of iridescent purple along its crest. (Kilgo 1988)

Another unique aspect of wood duck anatomy is that the female is far more colorful than are most other female ducks. The following are descriptions of adult hen mallards and hen wood ducks, respectively, from Chapman (1907).

Mallard Hen: Top and sides of head streaked with fuscous and buffy; back fuscous, and feathers with internal rings or loops and sometimes borders of pale ochraceous buffy; speculum as in preceding [male]; breast and belly ochraceous buffy, mottled with dusky grayish brown.

Wood Duck Hen: Throat and a stripe from the eye backwards white; crown purplish brown; sides of the head ashy brown; breast and side grayish brown streaked with buffy; belly white; back olive-brown glossed in greenish; inner primaries tipped with greenish blue.

The wood duck hen has more color and more iridescence than any other female duck. *Photo courtesy of Carrol Henderson.*

Descriptions of most hen ducks resemble Chapman's of the mallard, using words that are just variations on or shades of brown. It's rare to see words such as white, purplish, greenish, or blue in descriptions of hen ducks of any species. The "-ish" Chapman refers to is undoubtedly a reference to the iridescent qualities of these colors.

> As vividly as the wood duck drake stands out against this pin oak pond, I think the muted beauty of the hen creates an equal magic in the eye of the beholder. (Frank 1982)

> Where ducks are concerned, the most beautiful site that I have seen was when a female Wood Duck walked into the sun and all the iridescent colors on her appeared as if they were on fire. This occurred while I was just a few feet away, and the only word that can really describe it is *awesome*. (LeMaster 1985)

Colorful, long, and other remarkable feathers nearly doomed many species. In the late 1800s, it was fashionable to decorate women's hats with feathers, wings, and sometimes entire stuffed birds. Chapman (1886) reports on "two late afternoon walks through the uptown shopping district" of New York. He counted 700 ladies wearing hats, and 542 of those hats had parts of birds from forty different species.

Another report from that same year titled "Destruction of Birds for Millinery Purposes" supplies more numbers (Anonymous 1886). In one case, the report notes more than 70,000 skins were delivered to New York hatmakers from one village over a four-month period. Another party is said to have supplied 40,000 tern skins from Cape Cod in one season. Because these birds would have been harvested with guns, conservationists speculated about how many birds were killed to obtain that many useable skins, since many feathers were probably damaged by bird shot or too bloodstained to use. The millinery trade and feather-adorned hats incited deep passions among early conservationists. Celia Thaxter (1886) wrote of the results of her conversation with a woman wearing a feather-covered hat in an essay titled "Women's Heartlessness": "The woman went her way, a charnel-house of beaks and claws and bones and feathers and glass eyes upon her fatuous head." Later in the same essay Thaxter writes about the birds on those hats: "Do I not see you every day, your mocking semblance writhing as if in agony round female heads,—still and stark, sharp wings and tail pointing in stiff distress to heaven, your dried and ghastly head and beak dragged down to point to the face below, as if saying, '*She* did it.' The albatross of the Ancient Mariner is not more dreadful."

In addition to hats, wood duck feathers have been and continue to be put to other creative uses. The same brightly patterned feathers that attract female woodies can also be irresistible to some fish when properly presented to them. With some careful selection and manipulation of the feathers, those colors and patterns can be used to mimic the wings and bodies of the insects that trout, salmon, and other fish prefer. Or they may be just flashy and attractive enough to catch the eye of a passing fish.

> [T]heir feathers, which are exported to England, where the brilliant hues of part of their plumage are used in the manufacture of artificial flies for salmon and trout fishing. (Bogardus 1878)

> The Wood Duck has always been persecuted by man, not alone of its flesh, which is good, but for its feathers which are used in the making of artificial trout flies. (Kortright 1943)

> A wood duck skin became the valued possession of every serious fly dresser. The barred flank feathers, sometimes called "flytiers' gold," are still used to create enticing lures. . . . (Reeves 1988)

> Visible pain is scrawled on the expression of fly fishermen who learn that duck hunters . . . will frequently pluck and throw away the feathers of the wood duck. . . . (Reiger 2000)

Form can follow function in more ways than one.

Wood duck feathers have always been popular with people who enjoy fly fishing, especially those who tie their own flies. These are the Quill Gordon, Royal Coachman, a Celebrated Claret Fly, and Another Great Beauty. *Photo courtesy of Dave Krohne.*

The followers of Isaac Walton [fly-fishermen and -women] are generally much more familiar with this fowl than the professed sportsman, as they, in the pursuit of their favorite amusement, spend much of their time in the quiet and secluded haunts which these birds affect. (Lewis 1906)

The other point relevant to feather color is its biological or, more accurately, evolutionary purpose. The same issue arises when considering the large antlers of males of the deer family or the large or long feathers of some male birds, such as peacocks. We all learned growing up that female birds have muted colors so they are camouflaged as they sit on their nests. That's true. But the other reason is that they don't need to be flashy.

One very curious observation about the drake wood duck is that even though they are the most colorful ducks in North America, they can also be hard to see.

In spite of their size, they are difficult to see even in the bare trees where they blend with crooked limbs and other irregularities. (F. Leopold 1951)

The dense forests it frequented, its cryptic coloration in wooded and shadowed habitats, and its secretive nature served to limit the wood duck's visibility and relative importance in the eyes of early writers. (Reeves 1988)

The Wood Duck drake, with his iridescent green head, back, and tail feathers, blends into the background of a forest or the dark waters of a pond. (Shurtleff and Savage 1996)

How can something be bright and bold and flamboyant and gaudy, while also being cryptic and hard to see? This seeming ability to disappear most likely relates to some of the habitats wood ducks frequent.

[P]urling brooks flowing through dense woodlands where light and shade fleck the splashing waters, slow flowing creeks and marshy ponds—these are the haunts of the Wood Duck. (Forbush 1925)

For all its brilliant plumage, the male wood duck is amazingly camouflaged in its wooded habitats. Its many-angled "flowing" white lines break up its head and body shapes into fairly indistinct bits and pieces. . . . [I]n natural cover, the bold colors and patterns are broken up. Even with my telephoto lens, I often have difficulty locating them. (Bellrose et al. 1993)

We explain how something can be cryptically bold by starting with, of all things, the British Royal Navy during World War I. The British Navy was losing an unacceptable amount of shipping to German U-boats. No one can hide a large ship at sea. Ships were traditionally painted battleship gray in the hope that they would blend in with the sea and sky, especially in low light. They usually don't. Almost any ship seen against the horizon is going to be visible, especially if backlit and silhouetted by the setting or rising sun.

Several individuals came up with the idea of dazzle camouflage for large ships at sea. McRobbie (2016) writes that they "used broad swathes of contrasting colors—black and white, green and mauve, orange and blue—in geometric shapes and curves to make it difficult to determine the ship's actual shape, size, and direction." Behrens (2018) quotes a reporter who described a convoy of these dazzled ships as "barred, striped, blotched, smudged, ring streaked with vivid pinks, arsenic greens, violent blues." Rankin (2008) quotes an April 1917 letter to the British Admiralty from Norman Wilkinson, who wrote, "The proposal is to paint a ship with large patches of strong colour in a carefully thought-out pattern and color scheme." Do these descriptions sound somewhat like a certain duck? These painted shapes and colors were not intended to hide the ship. Indeed, they may have made the ship more visible in some situations. Rankin (2008) quotes a pamphlet published by the British military after World War I that stated "deception, not concealment, is the object of camouflage." The *Manual of Field Works (All Arms)*, published in 1921, defined camouflage as "the art of concealing that something is being concealed."

Merchant vessel dazzle-painted as seen through a submarine periscope.

The same vessel on identical course painted grey.

During the two world wars, some ships were painted in dazzle camouflage, making it more difficult for the enemy to determine the direction and speed of a moving ship.

To avoid detection, a ship can try to become invisible, which is almost impossible, or it can try to be unrecognizable, thus confusing the aim of whomever fires a torpedo at it. Disruptive colors and patterns don't make a ship invisible or hard to see, but they do make it difficult to determine how far away the ship is, the direction in which it is moving, and how fast it is going. Obviously all of those factors are critical if you are trying to sink a ship from a distance. As challenging as it can be to spot a wood duck, presumably in ideal light for photography, through a camera's telephoto lens mounted on a sturdy tripod and in the relative comfort of a blind, it's even more challenging to peer at a British warship in rough seas in poor light through the periscope of a U-boat.

A demonstration of this dazzle technique was given to King George V, a very experienced naval officer, and to a U.S. admiral. Both estimated the direction of the ship's travel incorrectly. The admiral blew up, shouting "How the hell do you expect me to estimate the course of a God-damn thing all painted up like that?" This, of course, was exactly the point and illustrated how difficult it would be to correctly aim a torpedo at a ship whose distance, direction, and speed could not be determined (Forbes 2009).

Where did this idea of disruptive camouflage come from? It came largely from nature. It was strongly advocated by two artists, father and son, Abbott and Gerald Thayer. The wood duck was one of the primary examples they used in promoting the principle. The Thayers studied camouflage in nature from their perspective as artists. They determined that animals concealed themselves in two ways. The first was obliterative camouflage, which allowed the animal to blend into the scenery, as a ruffed grouse or woodcock blended into the leaf litter on the forest floor. Many animals are lighter below and darker above; for example, many wild mammals have white bellies. Sunlight brightens the dark areas on top and shadows darken the light areas below, making the animal appear flat. This is often called countershading.

More importantly for our story, however, was the other type of camouflage the Thayers discussed: ruptive, or disruptive, camouflage. Thayer (1909) states that "'ruptive' markings, in general, are bold, massed patterns of contrasting shades and colors, disposed at seeming haphazard over the animal's body." The drake wood duck was one of their key examples of disruptive camouflage. It's interesting to consider how similar Thayer's descriptions of natural camouflage are to the idea behind ships' dazzle camouflage. *Ship Shape: A Dazzle Camouflage Sourcebook* is a collection of essays on World War I-era ship camouflage, which mentions the wood duck. Wood ducks are not subjects you typically see mentioned in a book on military strategy.

Abbott Handerson Thayer's 1909 painting of a wood duck concealed against a very specific background. *Image © Smithsonian American Art Museum. Gift of the heirs of Abbott Handerson Thayer.*

> In the marvelous completeness of this "vanishment," this "invisibility" in full and near view on quiet water, he is possibly unique among swimming birds. One may scan a Wood-Duck-haunted pool for many minutes, at close range, and fail to see the ducks that are floating on it. (Thayer 1909)

The reason the Thayers cite for this ability to disappear is the sun-dappled and visually complex forested wetland habitats wood ducks inhabit.

> Or, again, the white and dark marks, all together, suggest a definite fixed reflection-picture of a fringe of bushes along the shore, with the bright sky beyond cutting among their crowns. . . . (Thayer 1909)

Before dazzle camouflage was adopted by at least two powerful navies in the second decade of the twentieth century (the U.S. Navy also adopted the practice), disruptive camouflage had been the subject of some rancorous scientific debates in the previous decade. What really set off many scientists was the Thayers' description of flamingos. The Thayers argued that flamingoes were pink to camouflage them against the pink skies so common at sunset. Obviously, however, just like ships or any other backlit object, a pink flamingo would be silhouetted in black against a pink sunset.

Stephen Jay Gould's essay "Red Wings in the Sunset" gives a lengthy description of this debate. Although the Thayers are the subject of many scientific jokes and are often used in beginning biology classes as providing an example of bad science, Gould does vindicate them somewhat in his postscript to this essay, collected in his book *Bully for Brontosaurus* (1992). He quotes a letter from a naval officer who wrote, "Despite whatever everyone thought and thinks about Thayer's theories, both his 'protective coloration' and 'ruptive' designs were vital for concealing aircraft and ships."

One of the key players in this scientific debate was Theodore Roosevelt. In fact, he took time away from his presidential comeback campaign to write a hundred-page scientific treatise on the topic, something hard to imagine for modern politicians. He quickly focused on Thayer's wood duck paintings.

[Thayer's] pictures of wood-duck drakes, for instance, are designed to show that these birds are very inconspicuous, and so they are portrayed with the wood drake swimming among water lily blossoms, floating lily pads, brown sticks and the like, under circumstances that make the vivid coloring of the bird disappear. . . . As a matter of fact the circumstances under which the brilliant coloring of the wood drake tends to conceal him are wholly abnormal. . . . So far as it has any effect at all, the normal coloration of the wood drake is of a highly advertising quality. . . . (Roosevelt 1911)

Needless to say, Roosevelt was not a person to provoke into a war of words. His phrase "highly advertising quality," however, leads us to a much more scientifically rigorous explanation of the wood duck drake's bright colors, as well as of the colors of the males in so many other bird species.

In the bird world, it's almost always lady's choice when it comes to selecting a mate. Males can't choose; they can only be chosen. To be chosen, they need to be bigger, brighter, louder, flashier, or otherwise just more impressive than all the other males. Imagine long ago that all males were dull. (Female readers can pause here to insert their own joke before proceeding . . . .) They were all dull, but there was variation. Variation, as Charles Darwin describes in *The Origin of Species* (1859), is the foundation of evolution. He writes, "These individual differences are of the highest importance for us, for they are often the materials for natural selection to act on."

Imagine a pond with several drakes and hens on it. No two males are identical, and some may look more attractive, flashier or brighter, to the females than the others. More females select these brighter males to mate with. In the next generation, the males will be just a little brighter than the last generation. And, again, there will be variation. In this generation, the hens will preferentially select the brightest of the brighter males. Each generation, more females select the flashier, or sexier, males. With each generation, the males get flashier or brighter by this simple process. The occasional beneficial genetic mutation may briefly accelerate the process. After thousands of generations of evolution at work, we eventually have brightly colored wood duck drakes, peacocks with very long tails, songbirds with very loud songs, or bull elk with ridiculously large antlers.

What do these bright colors and other flashy traits advertise? They may tell the females that those particular males are better at finding food or defending a food-rich territory. They may say that the male's immune system is better at fighting off infections or parasites (Hamilton and Zuk 1982). While other males are looking for food or fighting off diseases, this male can spend that energy investing in flamboyant ornaments. The female's offspring will inherit the male's strong genes and will themselves be strong.

Those bright colors may not be the best thing for survival. Yes, they attract the ladies. But they may also attract the predators. In species like deer, growing a new set of antlers every year can be very stressful on the deers' bodies. Being big or bright or loud may not be best for your own survival. But it may be the best way for your genes to survive into the next generation.

This process is called sexual selection, and it was first described by Charles Darwin in *The Descent of Man and Selection in Relation to Sex* (1871). In many cases, sexual selection seems to run counter to the more familiar process of natural selection. Darwin wrote that "the males have acquired their present structure, not from being better fitted to survive in the struggle for existence, but from having gained advantage over other males." A few pages later he states that "hence it is the males that fight together and sedulously display their charms before the females."

Displaying your ornaments to the ladies may be even more effective than fighting to impress the ladies. Darwin writes, "From the foregoing facts we clearly see that the plumes and other ornaments of the males must be of the highest importance to them; and we further see that beauty is even sometimes more important than success in battle." Fighting is dangerous. The three options are (1) winning, (2) being injured, or (3) being killed. Or you could win but still be injured. In other words, if you want to display your evolutionary fitness and win the attention of a lady, it might be better to look tough and act tough than to be tough.

Another consideration regarding feathers is the mechanics of how birds grow them. Feathers are not living tissue, like skin. They are dead, like hair or fingernails. As such, they wear out and need to be replaced. Everyone is familiar with the general phenomenon of songbirds changing their feathers. Males have bright colorful plumage in the summer but duller colors in the winter. Females have duller-colored feathers year-round, but their feathers too wear out and need replacing.

For these reasons, brightly colored feathers have traditionally been called summer or breeding plumage and the duller feathers winter plumage. Birds molt from dull (winter plumage) to bright (summer or breeding plumage) in the spring and from bright to dull in the fall. That works for the songbirds most of us in North America are familiar with. The fall molt explains why many birding field guides have a page or two devoted to "confusing fall warblers." For many birds with different life histories, migration patterns, and habitats, however, that naming system for molting doesn't work at all.

Studying how birds molt their feathers and the feathers themselves has almost become its own field of science. Pyle (2005, 2008) and Howell (2010) provide a comprehensive review of molts and plumages. These researchers use words and phrases such as juvenile, formative, supplemental, prebasic, basic, prealternate, alternate, preformative, formative, definitive, simple basic, complex basic, simple alternate, and complex alternate. Modern scientists no longer use such terms as breeding, summer, or winter plumage. Sibley et al. (2001) state that "molt can be a fascinating, confusing, or just downright annoying topic, depending on your perspective," while Howell (2010) describes molts and plumages as "a bewildering subject."

To get away from the terms "breeding" and "winter" plumage, Humphrey and Parkes (1959) developed a new system for identifying feathers and molts that can be applied to all families of birds in all habitats. For adult birds, they developed the terms "basic" and "alternate." While many people simply substitute "basic" for "winter" and "alternate" for "breeding," that really isn't the intent. That terminology may work for most North American songbirds, but waterfowl are often cited as prime examples of the principle that breeding and summer plumages aren't always the same thing.

Howell (2010) writes, "Looking at duck molts opens up a Pandora's box of fascinating but often unanswered questions." Kortright (1943) writes, "In the early summer, as soon as the females are well established in their incubation duties, the males of most ducks . . . proceed to moult their bright winter plumage." Northern hemisphere ducks are one of the few groups of birds that have "bright winter plumage."

Ducks do it a little differently in a couple of ways. First, most birds molt their flight feathers one or two feathers at a time. That way, they always have the ability to fly. Most waterfowl will molt all their flight feathers at once during their early summer molt, becoming flightless for a couple weeks each summer as new feathers grow in. This molt from alternate to basic plumage, going from bright to dull feathers, is a complete molt. The ducks will eventually molt all their feathers.

Once the hens are on the nest, the males of most species congregate on large bodies of water, often called molt marshes, where they can relatively safely lose their feathers, including flight feathers, and molt into a drab plumage. In ducks, this is called the eclipse plumage. Wood ducks are a little different. Grice and Rogers (1965) hypothesize that drakes go to swamps and marshes where they hide in the thickest cover they can find. As evidence, they describe seeing many feathers, but rarely any actual ducks. Hens also molt their flight feathers all at once while their ducklings are too young to fly and the hens need to be always near them.

Hunters in northern-tier states are familiar with harvesting "eclipse drakes" in the first weeks of the duck hunting season. Both males and females will molt their body feathers at this time, but they won't lose or replace them all at once. The fall molt, going from eclipse or basic plumage to brighter or alternate plumage, is an incomplete molt; the ducks keep their wing feathers and flight ability but molt their body feathers.

The male ducks only keep their drab eclipse plumage for a few weeks in mid-to-late summer. Most ducks pair in the fall during the migration or on their wintering grounds. Male ducks molt back into their alternate plumage in the fall so they can look their flashiest and sexiest in the fall and winter. They keep these bright feathers through the spring and into early summer.

Using the traditional naming system associating summer with bright feathers and winter with dull feathers creates lots of trouble when considering waterfowl. Males develop their bright "summer" plumage in the fall to be used during the winter and have their drab "winter" plumage for a few weeks at the peak of summer. Howell (2010) writes that "much remains to be learned about a group as 'well studied' and familiar as ducks."

3 the acorn duck

The wood-duck is always a splendid table bird, and when it is fattened on wild rice and acorns is exceptionally fine.—*Huntington 1903*

Whenever present in the feeding grounds of the wood duck, duckweeds are probably its favorite food.—*Mabbott 1920*

Wild rice is available for only a short period during early autumn. . . . However, when available, wood ducks appear to feed upon the fruits of this plant almost to the exclusion of other foods.—*Coulter 1957*

Acorns are the favored foods of more wood ducks in more places than any other plant food.—*Bellrose 1976*

Scientists consider a number of issues when conducting dietary studies, simply because diet can be measured so many ways. Scientists can measure the volume of different types of food in the gut. They can count the number of individuals identified as eating a particular type of food. They can examine the relative caloric value of foods. They can measure the protein, carbohydrate, or fat/lipid content of each type of food. They might also study the time it takes an individual to find, eat, and digest different types of food.

Researchers can also examine food selectivity. If a food makes up 50 percent of the available foods in a habitat, for instance, and also makes up 50 percent of an animal's diet, researchers can conclude that the animals may be eating the food opportunistically or that they aren't selecting for or against it. Alternatively, if the habitat includes two foods in equal proportions, but birds eat 90 percent of one and only 10 percent of the other, we can conclude that they are selecting for one food type and against the other food type.

Feeding can also be studied in several ways. One method is to watch individual birds and record what they eat over a set period of time. This obviously creates several problems for the wildlife researcher. From an agricultural perspective, watching chickens or calves eating in a pen, their natural environment, is pretty easy. Wildlife biologists have it much worse. Imagine observing a duck tip up or skim the surface in the spring, presumably eating aquatic invertebrates. Watching through binoculars or a spotting scope from a distance that won't interfere with the duck's behavior will make it nearly impossible to tell what invertebrates it is eating. This method also requires that scientists be able to measure what foods are available in the bird's habitat, which can be very challenging.

Another method depends on keeping wild birds in captivity and doing feeding trials. In these experiments, researchers can give the birds exact amounts of different foods and then measure consumption by noting what is left after a period of time. Scientists can also measure preference by offering the birds different foods. These studies are informative, but obviously somewhat artificial.

One of the easiest ways to study diet in most species of wildlife is to harvest individuals and study the contents of their stomachs and digestive tracts. The gizzard of a wood duck is capable of grinding up acorns and pecans. Imagine what it does to small soft seeds or the bodies of tiny aquatic invertebrates. This grinding action of course presents additional challenges to dietary studies.

All foods are not created equal. Each type of food has carbohydrates, fats, and protein in different ratios, not to mention varying amounts of vitamins, minerals, and micronutrients. Bellrose and Holm (1994) provide a table of fifteen plants and nine invertebrates. Protein in plants, as a percentage of dry weight, ranged from 3.8 percent in water oak acorns to 29.2 in maple seeds. Among invertebrates, percent protein ranges from 4.0 percent in isopods to 71.1 percent in water boatman. Fat content in invertebrates was as high as 27.6 percent in whirligig beetles. In plants, fat ranged from less than one percent in barnyard grass to 14.6 percent in water oak acorns.

In assessing diet, we also need to keep in mind the time of year and location. A wood duck in Maine in August will have a different diet than that same duck in Georgia in January. Migrating birds will need different amounts and types of food than birds on their summer or winter habitats. Hens laying eggs in the spring, fast-growing young ducklings in the summer, or adults molting their feathers have different diets than they will have the rest of the year.

Before getting into the complexities of the natural diet, we should consider the mixed observations of woodies feeding in agricultural fields. Drobney and Fredrickson (1979) found little evidence of soybeans in the wood duck diet even though soybean fields were common in their study area. However, Hawkins and Bellrose (1940) do report some wood ducks feeding in wheat and cornfields. Bellrose and Holm (1994) also list several reports as well as their own observations of wood ducks feeding in agricultural fields. They state that corn can be an important part of the diet of incubating wood ducks.

To assess the wood duck diet more broadly, we should start by simply dividing the diet into plant and animal sources. Working in Maine, Coulter (1955) found that in spring wood duck diets were roughly 91 percent plant and 9 percent animal. In the fall, he found that vegetation made up 95 percent of the diet.

Drobney and Fredrickson (1979) studied wood duck diets in Missouri. In the fall, a rough baseline, invertebrates made up 33 and 36 percent of the female and male wood ducks' diets, respectively. During the breeding season, invertebrates made up 34 percent of the males' diet. In other words, the males don't change their diet much. Invertebrate consumption by females, however, increased to 54, 79, and 43 percent invertebrates for the pre-egg-laying, egg-laying, and post-laying periods. Put another way, hens dramatically shift their diet to accumulate enough protein to lay their clutches of eggs. Drobney (1980) demonstrated that a hen would need to eat roughly 60,000 invertebrates to lay a clutch of twelve eggs. During egg-laying and incubation, hens lose about 21 percent of their body mass (Drobney 1982). In summary, based on food intake, reproduction is very stressful on the hens' body, but not so stressful for the drake.

It's not that simple though. Drobney and Fredrickson (1979) found at least thirteen families of insects in the wood duck diet, and each family might encompass dozens of species. They found at least fourteen species of plants. Coulter (1955, 1957) found similar results in Maine. McAtee (1939) identified fifteen types of plants in the wood duck diet. These figures do not take into account the "miscellaneous" category included in all these diet studies, which could account for dozens more plant and animal species. Mabbott (1920) did the most extensive study by far of waterfowl diets, examining 413 wood duck stomachs. He found at least 145 species of plants and 162 species of insects.

This brings us back to Drobney and Fredrickson's 1979 study of hens and drakes during the breeding season. They showed that hens ate more invertebrates than drakes, but also that they ate a greater diversity of invertebrates, hypothesizing that "from a nutritional standpoint, it would be advantageous for hens to select a more diverse diet to ensure a proper balance of essential nutrients to meet the demands associated with egg production."

Diversity and biodiversity are words often thrown around casually with little understanding of their meaning or implications. These studies collectively show how important a diverse diet is for wood ducks. Lacking diversity, the hens might breed later, lay fewer eggs, and by the fall fledge fewer offspring.

In the historic waterfowl literature, several species are referred to as rice ducks. In more current research literature, almost all the discussion on waterfowl and rice has to do with domestic rice grown in the Carolinas, the Mississippi Alluvial Valley, or the Central Valley of California. Surprisingly little in the modern scientific literature has been written about wild rice at the northern ends of the flyways. This food is critical, however, to woodies and a number of other ducks as well as to other wildlife.

They [wood ducks] were feeding on the wild rice, in company with immense flocks of Mallards, Widgeon, and Teal. (Baird et al. 1884)

Its seeds are fed upon by practically all the fresh water ducks, and it presents such an attractive source of food supply as to entice even the wood duck from its secluded haunts to the open marshes where the wild rice grows. . . . The stomach and gullet of one duck shot at Point Pelee, Ontario, contained no fewer than 1,200 seeds of wild rice, with remains of others. (Mabbott 1920)

To all things a season, and never was that truer than when it comes to food for wildlife. Several writers point out the dependence of wood ducks on both acorns and rice, among other foods. The same writers put qualifiers on those statements, though, highlighting the season being discussed.

In the fall it resorts to the great rice marshes, and while the rice lasts that seems to be the principal food. Later it takes to the oak groves about the streams and lakes and seems to be especially partial to the acorns of the burr oak. (Kumlien and Hollister 1903)

Later in the season the wild rice marshes are visited and many wild fruits such as grapes and berries are found on dry land. . . . The wood duck is particularly fond of acorns, chestnuts, and beechnuts, which it picks up on the ground in the woods, turning over the fallen leaves to find them. (Bent 1951)

When woodies do find wild rice marshes or stands of oaks, they are pulled as if by magnets. Strand (2007) recounts watching nine hundred woodies come out of a ten-acre wetland in central Minnesota at sundown.

In addition to wood duck, summer duck, and Carolina duck, another of the most common names for woodies is the acorn duck. Indeed, almost everyone who writes about wood ducks mentions their fondness for acorns.

They ran hither and thither beneath the trees, picking up the fallen acorns which form a considerable part of their food at certain times of the year. (Roberts 1932)

During a mast year, the ground can be carpeted with acorns.

Woodies prefer to find their acorns in shallow flooded swamps and over-
flow bottomlands. But if the ground is devoid of undergrowth, they may
seek acorns off the ground, in groves of pin and white oaks. (Bellrose 1976)

When they can, wood ducks will feed on acorns to the point of gluttony. Jarosz (1960) reported that a wood duck harvested in Minnesota had fifty-six
bur oak acorns in his throat and crop, which took up about 130 cubic cen-
timeters of space.

In the fall it feeds freely on acorns, with which its stomach is often found
stuffed full. (Baird et al. 1884)

Several of the stomachs containing acorns were crammed with them, the
gullet and gizzard of one from Arkansas containing 15 entire acorns of pin
oak, with fragments of one or two others. (Mabbott 1920)

. . . wherever oak trees occur near water, wood ducks sometimes forsake
available aquatic foods to feed avidly on acorns. (Coulter 1957)

This fondness for acorns isn't limited solely to wood ducks. Acorns are incredibly nutritious, and during mast years very abundant. Just ask any bear, deer, turkey, or grouse about the desirability of acorns. Even other ducks have a strong fondness for acorns. Bent (1951) states that "the gadwall can walk well on land, where it forages for oak mast in the woods . . . often a long distance from water." Likewise, McAtee (1939) writes that mallards also will forage in woodlands and have "been known to gorge on acorns to such an extent that they are unable to fly."

It's not just acorns on the ground that cause wood ducks to leave their ponds and creeks. Wood ducks can perch on tree limbs and vines.

> About the time of the first light frosts, the ducks are much in the vine-hung trees that overhang slow streams and ponds. The small wild grape is then the attraction. (Sandys 1905)

> Wood ducks will search for acorns in leaf litter on the forest floor, and even on limbs before the mast crop has fallen. (Brakhage 1966)

While searching the woods for acorns and grapes, they won't turn down other food sources.

> The food of the Wood Duck, or as it is called in the Western and Southern States, the Summer Duck, consists of acorns, beech-nuts, grapes, and berries of various sorts, for which they half-dive, in the manner of the Mallard for example, or search under the trees on the shores and in the woods, turning over the fallen leaves with dexterity. (Audubon 1840)

> It is particularly partial to chestnuts, beechnuts, and acorns of the burr and pin oak, which it swallows whole, turning over the leaves to find them . . . (Kortright 1943)

When an abundant food source is available, wood ducks as well as other species of wildlife will key in on that one source, whether it be acorns, rice, or something else. In other words, get it while the getting is good. Acorns offer a good place to start looking into the details of the wood duck diet. The first point to determine is what species of oaks are most common in wood duck habitat, what species generally grow in nearby habitats, and what species are most often found in forest types generally distant from wood duck habitats.

Not all acorns are equal. Some are larger, some smaller. Some have tougher or thicker seed coats, others have thinner coats. Water oak acorns have an average shell thickness that is 45 percent greater than that of willow oaks, while Nuttall oak acorns are 30 percent larger than willow oak acorns (Barras et al. 1996). These factors affect mechanical digestion. How difficult is it to swallow and then grind up each species of acorn? In addition, acorns of each type of oak have a different level of protein, fat, tannins, and other chemicals or nutrients. For instance, fat content in acorns can range from 6.7 percent in pin oaks to 14.6 percent in water oaks (Bellrose and Holm 1994). Acorn protein content in cherrybark oak is 44 percent higher than in Nuttall oak (Barras et al. 1996). Gross energy can vary by as much as 11 percent between pin oaks and cherrybark oaks (Kaminski et al. 2003). Acorns vary in chemical components as well. Oaks are famous for having tannins. These chemicals, and others, affect how easily wildlife can break down the food chemically to extract the nutrients from it. Tannic acid in willow oak acorns is 155 percent higher than in Nuttall oak acorns (Barras et al. 1996).

Barras et al. (1996) studied food choice in captive female wood ducks, offering them a selection from four different oak species. The researchers found that wood ducks strongly preferred willow oak acorns, ate cherrybark oak acorns in rough proportion to their availability, and showed little interest in water and Nuttall oak acorns. Of the four, willow oak acorns are the smallest, have the thinnest shells, and offer the greatest meat-to-shell ratio. These factors, taken together, probably made them the easiest to grind up mechanically in the digestive tract.

(*Facing page*) A narrow, slow-flowing creek with duckweed collected in the wild rice stubble and an overhanging bur oak create nearly ideal habitat for wood ducks.

What does all this mean? The perfect acorn—small, with a thin shell, and high in fat and protein but low in tannins—doesn't exist. In addition, the ecology of acorn production is such that oaks typically have mast years with high acorn production and non-mast years with little production. McQuilkin and Musbach (1977), for instance, found that pin oak acorn production varied from a low of 8,200 acorns to 445,000 per hectare in different years. While several theories attempt to explain this boom-and-bust reproductive strategy, scientists have not zeroed in on an exact cause or causes. In fact, they haven't even determined if the variation is internally driven by genetics or externally driven by weather and related factors (Kelly and Sork 2002; Koenig et al. 2015). As with many natural processes, it probably depends on some of each. Importantly, different species of oaks will mast in different years. Allen (1980) found that 1972 was a high-yield year for white oak acorn production but a low-yield year for water and willow oaks. Conversely, in 1973 and 1974 water and willow oak acorn production was high, while white oak acorns were scarce.

What this means for the food supply for wood ducks, as well as mallards, turkey, grouse, deer, bear, and an array of other wildlife species that feed on acorns, is that forests should be managed or planted with a range of oak species native to that area and soil type. If one species fails to mast in one year, another species may do so. This suggests that some oak production will occur most years, even if it the species is not the favorite or most nutritious type of acorn from the perspective of each wildlife species depending on it. This is yet another practical application of biodiversity.

4 cavities and boxes

[I]t is not unusual for persons residing in suitable situations to invite its presence by preparing boxes and other convenient places for it to nest.—*Baird et al. 1884*

Many other kinds of wildlife depend on tree diseases. My pileated woodpeckers chisel living pines, to extract fat grubs from diseased heartwood. My barred owls find surcease from crows and jays in the hollow heart of an old basswood; but for this diseased tree their sundown serenade would probably be silenced. My wood ducks nest in hollow trees; every June brings its brood of downy ducklings to my woodland slough.—*A. Leopold 1949*

. . . [Nest boxes] serve a purpose out of proportion to their numbers because they have been the chief source of abundant and carefully documented knowledge about the Wood Duck—knowledge that would not be available through studies of natural cavities, which are extremely difficult to locate and monitor.—*Shurtleff and Savage 1996*

We suggest that adding artificial nest sites to areas where maturing forests are located near suitable foraging and brood-rearing habitats may do little to enhance carrying capacity and increase local abundance of wood ducks.—*Roy Nielsen et al. 2007*

While many ducks nest on the ground in the Prairie Pothole Region of the northern prairie states and southern Prairie Provinces or across the Canadian and Alaskan tundra, wood ducks nest in trees across much of the United States, although they are far more common in the eastern half of the country.

Many grouse, shorebirds, waterfowl, and songbirds nest on the ground across the treeless grassland and tundra regions of all continents. Even some forest songbirds, such as the golden-winged warbler and ovenbird, nest on the ground. Ground nesting makes a bird vulnerable to a number of factors. Nest predation can be high, as literally any predator can stumble onto the nest just walking by. Hailstorms can crush eggs or kill hens on the nest. Thunderstorms can flood nests. Wildfires or prescribed burns can destroy nests. Fortunately, most birds are good renesters if a nest is destroyed.

In grassland or tundra, a bird can nest on the ground. In the forest, birds can nest on the ground or in the shrub layer, subcanopy layer, canopy, where the branch meets the trunk of the tree, near the tip of the branch, or in between any of these. Many birds specialize, nesting on very specific structures within each of these groups or on specific tree species. The forest offers many places to nest.

Birds can also nest in the cavities of large trees, where they are protected from rain, storms, and wind. Loss to weather, predators, and other factors can still be high, however. Collias (1964) gives one of the most complete reviews available of the evolution of bird nests. One of the first facts he notes is that cavity nesting has evolved repeatedly in many groups of birds. Indeed, about half of the orders of birds recognized by modern taxonomists contain cavity nesting species. Cavities both supply shelter and conserve energy, presumably because they may provide some insulation from temperature swings. Collias states that cavities are beneficial to altricial species, but he doesn't mention precocial species. Altricial birds spend a significant amount of time as nestlings, as most songbirds do. Precocial species, such as grouse and ducks, leave the nest as soon as possible after hatching.

While cavity nesting has benefits, it also has drawbacks. If a species nests on the ground or builds a nest among the branches or twigs of a tree or shrub, the options for locating a nest are virtually unlimited, even considering that most species will seek preferred microhabitats when nesting. Cavities are often few and far between, however. Among the feathered, furred, and scaled, competition can be fierce for the prime real estate of a cavity.

Wood ducks aren't particularly choosy about the species of tree they nest in, as long as the tree is big enough and has a suitable cavity. Soulliere (1988) surveyed the literature and found at least forty-two species of trees mentioned as providing potential nesting cavities for wood ducks. It makes sense that a relatively large bird such as a wood duck would need a relatively large cavity, which of course requires a relatively large tree. Relatively speaking. Obviously, tree species that are more common in woodlands near rivers, creeks, lakes, or wetlands will be more commonly used. Soulliere (1988) found the average size of trees used by wood ducks to be twenty-three inches in diameter.

Researchers have found that the cavities in these older trees need to be about ten inches in diameter to suit wood ducks (Gigstead 1938; Bellrose 1953). An inch or more of wood on either side of the cavity is necessary as well, making the minimum diameter of the tree around thirteen or fourteen inches.

How high in the tree should these cavities be? Cavities can form (and nest boxes can be hung) anywhere from a few feet off the ground to the tops of the tallest trees. Do wood ducks have a height preference? Soulliere (1988) found, across fourteen studies, that the average height of a nesting cavity used by wood ducks was twenty-four feet, but the heights of cavities wood ducks would use ranged widely. Bellrose and Holm (1994) found that cavities above thirty feet were more acceptable than those at lower heights. Bowers and Atkins (1988), on the other hand, looked at nest boxes hung at 6.5, 12.5, and 18.5 feet above the ground and found occupation of the lowest boxes was twice that of either of the higher boxes.

How far from water will wood ducks nest? While most nests are found within two hundred yards or so of water (Grice and Rogers 1965), some can be a mile or more away (Bellrose 1953).

Finally, how common are natural cavities in the forest? That's a trickier question than it seems. What kind of forest? Upland or floodplain, dense or open, mature or regenerating from a natural disturbance or clear-cut, northern or southern latitudes? What species of trees are prevalent? Generally, cavities are relatively few and far between, although the exact density varies from site to site. Researching at Noxubee National Wildlife Refuge in Mississippi, Lowney and Hill (1989) found that 60 percent of the suitable cavities were in sycamore and beech trees, although those two species accounted for only 2.6 percent of the trees in the forests they studied. Similarly, Weier (1966) determined that black gum was the best tree for cavities at Mingo National Wildlife Refuge in Missouri, but that these trees were only a minor component of the forest. More generally, cavities at Mingo were described as "extremely scarce," and Noxubee was said to have a "paucity of suitable cavities."

And wood ducks require not just any cavity. It should be big enough, but not too big. It should be deep enough, but not too deep. If the hole is too small, the hen won't be able to enter. If the hole is too big, raccoons can easily get to the hens and eggs. Finally, the tree needs to be relatively close to water. Not a lot of trees are going to have cavities possessing all those characteristics.

Wood ducks must deal with intense competition for nesting cavities. Cavities and nest boxes are valuable real estate for a variety of wildlife. Many songbirds, including several woodpeckers, house wrens, tree swallows, bluebirds, great crested flycatchers, chickadees, nuthatches, and others nest in cavities. Most of these species will pick cavities too small to compete with wood ducks, but some may nest in cavities big enough for wood ducks.

Birds of prey such as kestrels, screech owls, and saw-whet owls will also nest in cavities. They may compete for wood duck–sized cavities. Common mergansers, hooded mergansers, buffleheads, and goldeneyes are all waterfowl that nest in wood duck–sized cavities.

Longley (1993) lists nineteen species of birds besides wood ducks that use wood duck nest boxes, as well as eight species of mammals, three species of snakes, and two invertebrates. We can assume these species would also compete for natural cavities. In my survey of the literature, I found eighteen mammals, two invertebrates, twelve mammals, and two snakes listed as either competitors for nest sites or nest predators. Bonar (2000) listed eighteen species of wildlife that nested in pileated woodpecker cavities. Frank (1948) found wood duck nest-box occupancy ranged from 4 to 11 percent, while gray squirrel occupancy ranged from 57 to 67 percent. McLaughlin and Grice (1952) found that 35 percent of their nest boxes were used by wildlife other than wood ducks. To summarize, not many natural cavities or nest boxes are out there, and competition is strong for those that are.

In "A Mighty Fortress" (1949), Aldo Leopold lists a number of species that make homes in his woodlot because of all the cavities in his injured, diseased, and dying trees: raccoons, ruffed grouse, wild [honey] bees, rabbits, chickadees, and wood ducks. It makes sense for Leopold to end his essay with the colorful wood duck, but he goes one step further. "The real jewel of my disease-ridden woodlot is the prothonotary warbler. He nests in an old woodpecker hole . . . the flash of his gold-and-blue plumage amid the dank decay of the August woods is in itself proof that dead trees are transmuted into living animals, and vice versa. When you doubt the wisdom of this argument, take a look at the prothonotary."

Hooded mergansers have been known for decades to nest in wood duck boxes, with hens of both species often producing mixed broods. In 1987, Marty Stouffer titled one of the episodes of his PBS television series *Wild America* "Woodies and Hoodies." At the northern edge of the wood duck's range, two other duck species readily take to nest boxes: the bufflehead (Gauthier 1988; Evans et al. 2002) and the common goldeneye (Zicus and Hennes 1989; Savard and Robert 2007).

Goldeneyes are a boreal forest species, nesting across the northern extents of Europe, Asia, and North America. In some areas, however, the goldeneye range overlaps with wood ducks. In New Brunswick, Prince (1968) determined that while wood ducks and common goldeneyes may nest in the same general areas, their microhabitats were different enough that interference or competition between them for nest cavities was slight. Strand (2006) built nest boxes with the same dimensions as a wood duck box but with a hole size of 3.5 by 4.5 inches, a half-inch wider in both dimensions than a northern Minnesota woody box. He has talked to other biologists, however, who have seen goldeneyes using wood duck boxes with the standard-sized opening.

The bufflehead is slightly smaller than the wood duck. Like the goldeneye, buffleheads are diving ducks that primarily nest in the boreal region. Agassiz National Wildlife Refuge in northwestern Minnesota saw its first bufflehead brood in 1985. From 1990 to 1997, buffleheads made up 1.0 to 1.7 percent of the diving duck broods seen on the refuge. From 2007 to 2011, they made up 20 to 40 percent of the refuge's diving duck broods. The 2007 Habitat Management Plan for the refuge notes the reason for this increase: it "coincides with aspen stands maturing beyond seventy years of age" (Ronning 2011; Ellis-Felege et al. 2018). Fortunately, like woodies, hoodies, and goldeneyes, buffleheads will readily accept nest boxes (Corrigan et al. 2011). Bahls and Bartholmai (2013) recorded buffleheads nesting in boxes at Horicon Marsh in Wisconsin. Their observations are noteworthy for a couple of reasons. First, Horicon is well south of the traditionally recognized breeding range for this species. Second, they recorded a bufflehead hen who successfully incubated and hatched a brood of seven bufflehead and four wood duck ducklings. As goldeneyes may prefer a slightly larger hole in the nest box, nest boxes designed for buffleheads can use a three-inch round hole.

Cavities form naturally in almost all large trees. Damage from a broken branch, freezing, lightning, fires, or floods can cause weak spots in trees that allow infections by bacteria and fungi to enter, eventually turning a wound into a hollow cavity.

> It was an old, grotesque white oak, whose top had been blown off in a storm. . . . In this hollow and broken top, and about six feet down, on the soft, decayed wood, lay thirteen eggs. . . . (Wilson 1839)

> [T]hey resort more commonly, I think, to partly hollowed red maple, oak, and other trees where a large branch at some time has been torn away. . . . (Phillips 1925)

Being hollow often doesn't weaken the tree. In a tree trunk, the only living tissue is a layer a few cells thick called the cambium, lying just under the bark. The wood and bark are dead material. The light sapwood just beneath the bark does help with water transport, but the darker heartwood in the center of the trunk doesn't do much for the tree. In fact, if a heavy limb does break off or a trunk becomes hollow, it could in some cases help the tree structurally, as it no longer needs to support the weight.

Some writers describe woodies as nesting in abandoned woodpecker holes, specifically made by ivory-billed and pileated woodpeckers.

> There is no doubt that, without pileated woodpeckers, we wouldn't have nearly the number of wood ducks that exist and thrive today.
> (Bellrose et al. 1993)

James Tanner's *Ivory-billed Woodpecker* (1942), the definitive resource on ivory-bills, described the primarily southern ivory-billed habitat: "In the Carolina and Georgia regions, most of the Ivory-bill records are along the Pee Dee, Santee, Savannah, and Altamaha Rivers. . . . Almost all of the Ivory-bill records in the Mississippi Delta occur in the first bottoms outside of the backwater and swamp areas. . . . Ivory-bills in Florida frequently fed in the pine woods bordering the swamps." Large trees near, adjacent to, or in swamps and rivers sounds like ideal wood duck habitat. The same logging that impacted wood ducks, however, also impacted these large woodpeckers.

To add insult to injury, woodpeckers were even hunted for food in the late 1800s. In his book *In Search of the Ivory-Billed Woodpecker*, Jerome Jackson (2004) quotes one source as saying that "its flesh was said to be quite palatable, and since it was a large bird, it was consistently shot for food," while another source states that ivory-bills "were shot for food, and the people—the crackers—consider them 'better than ducks.'"

Deforestation together with hunting hit woodpecker populations hard. In fact, the last ivory-billed was seen in the wild in 1944, and they are almost surely extinct now. In *The Grail Bird*, Tim Gallagher (2005) states that "by 1920, no one had seen any ivory-bills for several years, and many ornithologists believed that the species was extinct." That's roughly the same time people were worried about wood ducks going extinct. The loss of big trees and woodpeckers to make holes in those trees may have been doubly impactful on wood ducks.

The pileated is the smaller cousin of the ivory-billed woodpecker and probably suffered similar declines. This bird has recovered, however, and is now relatively abundant. Breeding Bird Survey data from the top seven wood duck harvest states illustrates the population increase over the last fifty years. Comparing five-year averages of pileated woodpeckers seen per survey route from 1967 to 1971 and 2013 to 2017, pileated woodpeckers increased 20 percent in Arkansas, 31 percent in Louisiana, 41 percent in South Carolina, 107 percent in Georgia, 269 percent in North Carolina, 279 percent in Wisconsin, and 506 percent in Minnesota. This may simply indicate, however, that forests are maturing and trees are getting larger.

In many cases, a combination of factors produces the cavity. A woodpecker, even the smaller downy or hairy woodpecker, initiates a hole, which then becomes big enough for a wood duck through the process of infection and decay. Often woodpeckers will find points of infection where the wood is softer to begin their excavations. The relative importance of holes created by "natural" damage to the trees and those holes created by woodpeckers is questionable, however, and probably varies from location to location.

If it cannot find a natural cavity that suits its taste, the wood duck occasionally occupies the deserted nesting hole of one of the larger woodpeckers, such as the ivory-billed or pileated woodpecker, or even the flicker. (Kortright 1943)

Deserted pileated woodpecker (*Hylatomus pileatus*) nest sites account for relatively few of the available cavities studied, but they may be important because of their proportionately high use rate by wood ducks. (Soulliere 1988)

Pileated woodpeckers and fox squirrels provide cavities that occasionally are used by wood ducks, but most cavities of sufficiently large size develop from heartwood decay, with wind breaking away a large branch or the top of a trunk to expose the interior of the cavity to the outside. (Bellrose et al. 1993)

Weier (1966) studied nesting trees in Missouri and found that 61 percent of the cavities were the result of a broken or dead limb; 18 percent were due to fire scars; and lightning and logging operations caused 8 percent of the cavities. Only 4 percent of the cavities were formed by woodpecker activity.

Collectively, these observations led people to decide they could make structures specifically for wood ducks. We can complicate the math behind the relative importance of cavities formed from broken limbs versus those formed by woodpeckers by introducing nest boxes built and hung by people. The wood ducks' willingness to nest in any structure, even if near people, was recognized early on.

> [A] large sloop lay on the stocks, nearly finished; the deck was not more than twelve feet distant from the nest, yet notwithstanding the presence and noise of the workmen, the Ducks would not abandon their old breeding place, but continued to pass out and in, as if no person had been near. (Wilson 1839)

> They nest in the cavities of trees and never on the ground, although sometimes they choose very peculiar situations, the most remarkable of which I have record being the individual that for several years built her nest in an unused stovepipe projecting from the side of a boat house. (Reed 1912)

Many people probably think that nest boxes for ducks were pioneered with the wood duck. Not true. Phillips (1925) cites several earlier writers who describe nest boxes for goldeneyes in Finland and Sweden in the early 1700s. These boxes were purely utilitarian. Chickens or other egg-laying birds don't do well in these northern climates. Scandinavians found they could encourage goldeneyes to nest in nest boxes and then harvest the eggs. In many cases, they could harvest twenty to thirty eggs from each box during the nesting season.

This in turn led to efforts to identify the best construction for nest boxes. What size hole is ideal for wood ducks? More generally, how deep should the box be, and how large should the floor area be? Nest boxes, artificial cavities, have been developed by studying natural cavities used by wood ducks.

The wood duck nest box has undergone significant changes over the last eighty years. People have used three basic materials to make boxes: wood, metal, and plastic. The first goal was obviously to make a box attractive to and likely to be used by wood ducks. The next requirement was to make the box as safe from predators as possible. The boxes also had to be durable, so that only occasional repairs or replacement are needed. The last goal was to make them inexpensive enough and easy enough to build that just about anyone could afford the materials and have the skills to build one. The modern designs are relatively inexpensive. In a fully equipped wood-working shop, one or two people could cut out and put together quite a few boxes in a weekend. But even those with only a handsaw and a drill can make a wood duck box.

Some of the first efforts described by Bellrose (1953) used slabs of wood with the bark still attached. Several hundred of these were used in Illinois in the late 1930s. This first effort had only a 12 percent occupancy rate, and only 30 percent of those produced ducklings. The builders learned several lessons from this. Many of the boxes had large cracks in the bottom and were too shallow. They were also hung in small trees in habitats in which the wood ducks probably weren't looking to nest. Last, these slab boxes were heavy and short-lived.

In 1940, Frank Bellrose and Art Hawkins measured the interior dimensions of 28 natural cavities. (In 1964, Bellrose et al. published further results from these measurements.) They found that the most popular cavities for wood ducks had openings of 10 to 19 square inches, a depth of 10 to 19 inches, and a floor area of 100 to 110 square inches. The authors then developed plans for a box using rough-cut lumber. The boxes had ten-by-ten-inch interiors and were twenty-three inches deep. A circular hole cut approximately eighteen inches from the bottom served as an entrance. They used cypress wood because it is durable and resistant to rot. In 1939, they built and hung 450 boxes and another 250 the following year.

They continued to refine their design, especially the shape and size of the entry hole. In 1941 they experimented with a three-and-a-half-inch round hole, a diamond shaped opening five inches wide by three inches tall, and a five-by-three-inch rectangle. Raccoons were able to easily fit through all these holes. The following year the diamond hole was reduced from five-by-three to four-by-three inches, and the proportion seemed to work well in excluding adult raccoons. They finally settled, however, on an elliptical hole four inches wide by three inches tall, the size still recommended today (Henderson 1992).

Squirrels were another problem for nesting ducks. A number of methods were tried to keep them away, including painting the tree above and below the nest box with Tanglefoot, a sticky substance meant to deter moth larvae from crawling up a tree. Next, a conical top was put on the roof to prevent squirrels from entering from above. A third attempt used metal flashing around the front of the box. All of these options made the boxes expensive and difficult to construct. In the end, they decided that the old realtor's adage "location, location, location" was probably the best way to attract wood ducks and to deter most predators.

In our experiments, the placement of nest boxes proved to be as important as their design and construction. (Bellrose 1953)

Researchers have also worked with galvanized metal and plastic houses. Plastic houses must be purchased premade, however, and metal can be more difficult to work with than wood. Today, most wood duck houses are still built with wood. Rough-cut cedar is often the wood of choice, especially in northern regions. In the South, cypress remains a very good option. Any rot-resistant wood will work, however. Earlier plans called for using twelve-inch-wide boards, but most modern plans say birds prefer boxes made with ten-inch-wide boards. These boards are also cheaper and lighter in weight, making it easier to hang them. Today, many wood duck nesting houses are mounted on poles or posts in the water or at the edge of the water. Often, a wide metal cone attached to the pole or post helps pre-

This nest box is mounted on a post and has a cone-shaped predator guard installed beneath it. *Photo courtesy of Carrol Henderson.*

vent predators from accessing the box from below. In other cases, a piece of sheet metal too slick for mammals or snakes to crawl over is tightly wrapped around the post.

Simply hanging nest boxes won't cure all the problems for wood ducks in an area. Just like us and all wildlife, wood ducks need several things: food, shelter, and habitat. In most cases, one of those factors will limit the population. If natural cavity nest sites are abundant in an area, simply adding more of an already plentiful resource won't help the ducks. If an area lacks wood ducks or has only a few, something other than nesting sites may be limiting the population.

My wood ducks doubtless nest in the hollow trees; at least they do not nest in the artificial houses I have put up, and every June brings its brood of downy ducklings to my woodland slough. (A. Leopold 1999)

Wood ducks are often seen among the trees along the edge of the marsh at Great Meadows where they perched on limbs and appeared to be searching for nest cavities. This indicates that, in spite of the many nest boxes available on the marsh, and the scarcity of natural cavities, they continue to search for nest sites in traditional locations. (Grice and Rogers 1965)

5 nesting

[W]hen entering the hole in which its nest is, the bird dives as it were into it at once, and does not alight first against the tree . . .—*Audubon 1840*

He can get into a very small hole, only a trifle larger than that used by a flicker, and, oddly enough, he can enter it at speed. I have seen them fly at the hole and just dash into it. —*Askins 1931*

. . . and then fly directly to the hole and plunge in. The wings close just as they hit the hole and there was an apparent drop down.—*Gigstead 1938*

It is possible, but only once.—*Breckenridge 2009*

Like many ducks, wood ducks court during the fall migration, arriving in their wintering habitat already paired. Armbruster (1982) recorded courtship displays in Missouri in late September. They may continue to court into the spring nesting season.

One would think that the bright feathers of the male would be all it would take to woo nearby females. But like almost all ducks, woodies have evolved a set of highly stylized displays to impress hens. As shown earlier, it's better to display than to fight. Ethologists, scientists who study animal behavior, have come up with fairly descriptive names for these behaviors. Armbruster (1982), Korschgen and Fredrickson (1976), and Frederickson (1988) list drinking, preen-behind-the-wing, burping, chin-lifting, turn-the-back-of-the-head, display shake, wing-and-tail-flash, bill-jerk, bill-dipping, facing, pseudo mock-preen, supplanting, and inciting as typical behaviors of displaying males. Korschgen and Fredrickson were also able to demonstrate that older males have more stylized displays than yearling males.

Observe that fine drake! how gracefully he raises his head and curves his neck! As he bows before the object of his love, he raises for a moment his silken crest. His throat is swelled, and from it there issues a guttural sound, which to his beloved is as sweet as the song of the Wood Thrush to its gentle mate. The female, as if not unwilling to manifest the desire to please which she really feels, swims close by his side, now and then caresses him by touching his feathers with her bill, and shews displeasure towards any other of her sex that may come near. Soon the happy pair separate from the rest, repeat every now and then their caresses, and at length, having sealed the conjugal compact, fly off to the woods to search for a large Woodpecker's hole. (Audubon 1840)

The gorgeously colored drake swims close to his modest little wife who is dressed in quaker gray and wears large white spectacles. If she swims too fast for him he is apt to touch her head with his bill, and when she stops he jerks his head up and down in an abbreviated bow. At the same time he whistles in a low sweet way as if he were drawing in rather than blowing out his breath. The feathers of his crest and head are at the same time erected. (Townsend 1916)

Once the drake and hen are paired, the drake will defend the hen against other males. He rushes toward the male with head lowered in a threatening manner, but the two males almost never come to blows, as the intruder quickly retreats. This is a good illustration of sexual selection as well as of Darwin's quote that "beauty is even sometimes more important than success in battle."

With the crest elevated, and like a coronet on his head which is drawn backward as proudly as the swan's, each male, an undisputed monarch of the mirror lake, glides here and there, in and out in his ingenious and undisguised endeavors to outdo every other in his imperial display. . . . (Hatch 1892)

A few lost feathers may be the extent of physical damage, but apparently this is sufficient to settle the question of competition for a specific mate. (Hester and Dermid 1973)

One of the best determinants of the success of a nesting box program is the success of breeding in the previous year (Bellrose 1953). Wood duck hens have a strong instinct to return to the nest where they were hatched, a phenomenon known as *philopatry*. Grice and Rogers (1965) found that 43 percent of the hens they captured in their study area had hatched there in a previous year. Hepp and Kennamer (1992) found that 42 percent of the hens in their study returned to the same box, and another 38 percent nested in a different box on the same wetlands. Thomforde (2014) recorded eight hens that had been captured in the same box the previous year. Five of those hens had been in the same nest box for two years, one had nested in the same box for three consecutive years, and two hens had maintained possession of boxes for four years straight. Wilson and Audubon hypothesized about this nest site fidelity in the early 1800s.

Wood ducks return early in the spring to the north, while others move hardly at all and nest anywhere suitable in the south. Regardless of where they nest, they generally start looking for cavities and boxes early in the spring. Since pair bonds occur several months before the nesting season, hens and drakes arrive at their nesting area ready to nest. The pair, led by the hen, fly through the forest looking for a likely cavity or nest box. They will often perch on a tree branch to more slowly and carefully inspect the immediate area. They may inspect several before they find one to their liking. The hen investigates closely while the drake stands guard on a nearby branch.

Once she selects a nest, the hen will begin laying eggs. She will lay one a day, usually in the morning. The drake will dutifully accompany the hen to the nest each morning and perch on a nearby limb. She will cover the egg with wood chips or any other loose material in the cavity before leaving. Starting around egg seven, or day seven, the hen will pluck some down feathers from her breast and will add more feathers with each day and egg. The average clutch is about twelve eggs. By the time the hen begins incubating the eggs, there may be two hundred cubic inches of fluffy down feathers insulating the eggs.

Over this period, the home range of the hen will be about 910 acres, or a little under a mile-and-a-half square (Hartke and Hepp 2004). Apparently it takes a large area for her to find the resources—the right quality and quantity of food—that she needs to lay her eggs. Throughout the egg-laying period, the hen will not incubate the eggs. For lack of a better term, the eggs are held in a state of suspended animation. If the hen started incubating the first egg immediately, the ducklings would hatch over a twelve-day period. The eggs must hatch at the same time so that the hen can leave the nest with all her ducklings at the same time. If she started incubating with the first egg, only one egg would hatch each day over an almost two-week period. The older ducklings would make noise, attracting predators.

Once she has laid her last egg, the hen begins incubation. Incubation lasts about thirty days, a few days longer than for many ducks. The hen leaves the nest for an hour or so early in the morning and again late in the afternoon and joins the drake on a nearby pond or creek to feed. When she leaves the nest, she carefully covers the eggs with down to keep them warm.

Up until the last few days of incubation, the drake will accompany the hen back to the nest before returning to a nearby pond or creek.

> The beauty of the flashing drake as he swings by, having escorted his lady home, is a charming memory for a winter evening. (F. Leopold 1951)

It's easy to romanticize this behavior and put it into human terms. We shouldn't do that. There are very practical reasons for the drake to remain nearby. If the nest is destroyed and the hen lays a second clutch of eggs, he will be ready to mate with her. If he had left, another male could mate with her, and he would leave no offspring. Toward the end of incubation, however, the drake will leave to molt. He is not abandoning his children: he's doing what's best for both him and them. He wouldn't be able to do

Eggs in the nest box covered with downy feathers from the hen.
Photo courtesy of Carrol Henderson.

much if he did stick around. He can't incubate the eggs, and he isn't much help raising the brood. Indeed, it is likely that all he would do would be to eat some of their food and draw attention to the helpless ducklings. Like all male ducks, the male wood duck finds it best to just leave the hen alone to raise her brood.

During incubation, the hen rotates two eggs every twelve hours from the edge of her nest to the center so that over the month-long incubation each egg receives the same amount of warmth from the hen's body to aid development.

Breckenridge (1956) used a pressure plate in three nest boxes to study the hen's activity pattern. He found that hens laid their eggs between five and eight each morning. The egg-laying period ranged from eight minutes to almost three-and-a-quarter hours, with an average of one hour and forty-eight minutes. The hen left the nest most mornings and evenings to eat and meet with her drake. Breckenridge found that the total time off the nest each day related to temperature. The cooler it was, the more time the hen spent in the nest incubating her eggs.

Breckenridge also used a thermocouple to measure the heat in the nest. Even covered with down, when the hen left the eggs on a sixty-degree day, they cooled by 13.5 degrees in eighty minutes. During these periods, we can assume embryo development slowed. It may be variations in periods like this that explain the range of hatching dates that some have observed.

Between the twelve-day egg-laying period and the thirty-day incubation period, the hen and her eggs are quite literally sitting ducks. The hen must deal with at least three issues during this period. Before the egg-laying starts, she must compete for cavities. Once she's incubating, predation becomes an issue, threatening both her and her clutch of eggs. The third issue is nest dumping, or nest parasitism.

In our culture, parasite is a loaded term with negative connotations. No one would think it a compliment to be called a parasite. When most people think of parasites, they think of something small crawling around inside another organism or of picking ticks off their pets in the spring. But the term means something very specific to biologists.

Nest parasitism is simply one hen, the parasite, laying an egg in the nest of another hen, the host, in the hopes that the host will raise the parasite's young. This is a phenomenon common among many birds. Often the parasite and host hen are of the same species, but not always. Cowbirds are famous, or infamous, nest parasites of songbird hosts. In the context of wood ducks, hooded mergansers are probably the most common parasite, after other wood duck hens. While the hen is away, another hen enters the cavity or nest box and deposits her own egg. The resident hen will then incubate and raise the duckling.

This is a good deal for the parasitizing hen. Someone else raises her ducklings at no cost to her. She can spread her eggs around several nests, so that even if one or two nests are destroyed by weather or predators, a few of her ducklings are likely to survive. In many cases, the parasite hen may go on to lay and incubate her own clutch. She has thus spread the risk by not putting all her eggs in one basket, or cavity, or box. Unfortunately, it's not that simple.

Nests can be parasitized by multiple hens. In several cases, researchers have found forty or more eggs in a single nest box. No hen can incubate all those eggs. She may only be able to incubate a percentage of those eggs, or she may abandon the nest completely, leaving all the eggs to die. Alternatively, other researchers have shown that parasitism can increase production from nests. This may be a matter of degrees. If the level of parasitism is low and the nest gets just a few extra eggs, the hen will be capable of incubating all the eggs. The box will eventually produce fourteen ducklings instead of twelve, for instance (Grice and Rogers 1965; Morse and Wight 1969; Heusman 1972; Clawson et al. 1979). If population density increases and multiple hens dump eggs in multiple nests, however, then hatchability decreases, since the hen simply can't incubate too many eggs. Semel et al. (1988) showed that as clutch size increased to up to fifteen eggs, hatchability increased. In clutches with sixteen to forty-four eggs, however, hatchability decreased as the number of eggs increased. Jansen and Bollinger (1998) found that hatchability in unparasitized nests was 91 percent, but in parasitized nests only 73 percent. Haramis and Thompson (1985) found that hatchability was lowest when population density was highest. In one year of their study, hatchability dropped to 32 percent. With nest parasitism, a little bit of a bad thing isn't too bad, but a lot of a bad thing can be pretty bad.

Simple math says that putting up more nest boxes creates more opportunities for more hens to produce more ducklings. More is always better than less. Logic states that given more nest boxes, each hen will select a box and start laying eggs. Hen density, nest-box density, and duckling density should all be highly correlated. Except . . . . Here's where biology and behavior start to overrule simple math. Wood duck hens don't simply respond to new boxes, they also respond for some reason to other hens. Something about watching one pair of wood ducks at a nest box seems to attract or stimulate other pairs. Often this crowding around single nest boxes would occur even if there were unoccupied nest boxes nearby.

> Often two pairs, and sometimes three, would try to inspect a nest box simultaneously. (Jones and Leopold 1967)

> Soon after sunrise each day, pairs of Wood Ducks began appearing near boxes. Pairs arrived singly, usually from different directions, and remained apart. If one female entered or left a box, however, a group of pairs quickly coalesced and more females sought to enter that nest. Pairs often flew considerable distances (e.g. 0.5-1.0 km) from vantage points high in trees to boxes where such activity was occurring. Soon the chosen box was surrounded by many birds (e.g. in one case 8 pairs), either on the water or perched on stumps or adjacent boxes. (Semel and Sherman 1986)

Several studies state that wood ducks seem to be very tolerant of other hens during the egg-laying period. That tolerance dropped dramatically once the hens starts incubating, however. Clawson et al. (1979) report a hen entering the nest box of another hen who was already incubating. The two hens fought so hard the box shook.

In many cases, nest parasitism, or nest dumping, is actually the population being a victim of its own success. As more hens are born in an area and return to the same area the next year, the local population will grow and competition will inevitably occur.

> [T]he use of boxes in any one year was determined largely by nest success in the unit in the previous year. (Bellrose 1953)

Haramis and Thompson (1985) and Jones and Leopold (1967) both demonstrated that nest parasitism increases as population density increased. An increased population is good up to a point. But if the population increases to the point where nest parasitism starts to negatively affect nest success, it's not as good. Good reproduction can literally be the victim of its own success in past years.

The spacing of nest boxes is probably one of the biggest contributions to nest parasitism. As noted, watching other hens enter a nest provided some stimulus to some hens to also enter and lay eggs. Reiger (1994) describes moving a box just thirty feet to be out of the line of sight from an adjacent nest box, thus fixing the problem. In many early nest box efforts, nest boxes were crowded into small areas. In some cases, nest box "condos" were built. This makes intuitive sense. If some nest boxes are good, more nest boxes are better. In the natural environment, however, cavities, even in pre-1800s forests, are available in relatively low density in any one area. Crowding nesting opportunities into a small area creates a very unnatural situation.

> Space houses according to habitat and potential breeding population. A desirable density appears to be two to three houses per acre for woodlots where nesting in natural cavities is at the rate of one pair per 10 acres. (Bellrose et al. 1964)

> Generally, fewer well-scattered boxes produce as many ducklings as highly clumped boxes and require less time for annual maintenance and repair. (Fuller 1975)

> Data we present suggest that to retain the advantages of using nest boxes to study and manage Wood Ducks, but to minimize the behavioral pathologies associated with dump nesting and high population densities, artificial nesting structures should be placed in visually occluded sites and at densities approximating those in which the species evolved. (Semel et al. 1988)

Nest parasitism was still a good strategy, for the parasite, back in those pre-logging day forests. Hens probably would have tried to visit their nest cavities discretely to avoid being detected by any hen happening by, and nest parasitism rates may have been lower. When nest boxes are crowded into an area, however, it's impossible for the hen to be cryptic and avoid parasitism. It hasn't been demonstrated conclusively, but high densities of nest boxes may also "train" predators such as raccoons to search for more nest boxes for an easy meal.

One reason, besides "more is better," for grouping nest boxes is that it's much easier and quicker for biologists to check clusters of nest boxes, as compared to checking the same number of boxes scattered over a large area. If clustering boxes affects reproduction, however, the boxes should be spread out.

> We hypothesize that proximity and visibility of nest boxes facilitates the development of supernormal clutches (i.e. dump nesting). The grouping of artificial structures forces Wood Ducks, which normally nest solitarily, into semicoloniality. (Semel and Sherman 1986)

Once the hen is on the nest and incubating her eggs, the hen has to worry about nest predators. Predators can include several species of snakes; birds such as flickers or woodpeckers, which will poke holes in eggs; and several squirrels, opossum, fisher, marten, mink, and rats. The predator that has received by far the most attention, however, is the raccoon.

Americans love to hate predators. It's a simple answer to a simple question. Predators kill prey. If we kill predators, there will be more prey for us to either watch or hunt ourselves. Paul Errington was an Iowa wildlife biologist who specialized in predator ecology. He responded to the idea of killing predators to produce more wildlife in his book *A Question of Values* (1987): "As reasoning, it provides us with a comfortable and satisfying panacea, but it has the often overlooked factual disadvantage that this is not the way things are apt to work out." The research on wood duck nest predation seems to mirror Errington's ideas.

> Predation did not appear to be excessive and no one species of predator, or type of predation, was obviously more important than any other. On the contrary, predation seemed to come from many different sources, each playing a relatively minor role. (Grice and Rogers 1965)

> While the percent of nests destroyed by predators is relatively low, problems stem from occupancy by other species of birds and insects. (Webster and McGilvrey 1966)

Back in the 1950s we thought the raccoon was primarily responsible for a large decrease in breeding wood ducks in the Midwest. Yet, today we find that raccoons are almost as abundant as they were then. (Bellrose 1966)

Predator control has a cultural context as well. In recent decades, fur has gone out of fashion. While many people will support conservation and habitat protection, support wanes among some when the image of conservation is a grinning individual holding a dead or bloody carcass. Trapping has always had its place in our rural culture and in wildlife management, but today it receives cultural scrutiny also. It can be frustrating for some people, but wildlife management doesn't happen in a vacuum. There is usually a cultural context.

Trapping wildlife can be a losing proposition in some cases. And it can be expensive. A raccoon that is trapped and removed will probably be replaced by another raccoon in a very short period of time. If, on the other hand, habitat management is conducted that creates habitat favorable to one species, wood ducks, and unfavorable to another species, raccoons, more people will support the effort, and it will be longer lasting. A good habitat management project can reduce predator populations for years to decades, while a trap only reduces the population for weeks to months.

In general, the most desirable form of control would be the use of devices or habitat manipulation aimed at placing wood ducks beyond the reach of predation rather than attempting to destroy the predator. (McGilvrey 1968)

Nest predation and parasitism are clearly related to forest habitats. Bellrose (1953) found that nest boxes in upland woods had a higher occupancy rate than boxes in floodplain forest. In Bellrose's study area, cavities were more abundant in the uplands, and raccoon density was lower in the upland forests as compared to floodplain forests.

Nest success appeared higher in floodplain (80%) than in upland (58%) forest, although the difference was not statistically significant, because we found so few floodplain nests. (Ryan et al. 1998)

Dozens of studies have been written on boxes versus cavities, high- versus low-density nest-box placement, predation, parasitism, and other factors, and many studies seem to disagree with others. Readers may find this frustrating. Can't scientists agree on anything? Consider the following pairs of seemingly contradictory quotations.

BROOD PARASITISM

When two or more hens attempt to use a single nest box, the probability of successful reproduction is greatly reduced. (Jones and Leopold 1967)

[D]ump nesting is beneficial to most wood duck populations. (Heusmann et al. 1980)

NEST BOX SPACING OR DISTRIBUTION

Erect houses in groups, to attract returning yearlings as breeding birds. (Bellrose et al. 1964)

In other words, the placement of boxes at high densities and in obvious places (a standard management practice) makes it difficult for females to visit their nests undetected. If the local population density rises due to successful reproduction and female philopatry, the effect is exacerbated, making it nearly impossible for females to hide their nest sites or to repel increasing numbers of potentially parasitic conspecifics. (Semel and Sherman 1986)

MOUNTING HEIGHT FOR BOXES

Place some nesting houses in each unit over 20 feet up in large trees (the higher the better) to secure optimum initial use. (Bellrose et al. 1964)

Manager need not strive to place wood duck boxes at extreme heights to increase use. . . . (Bowers and Atkins 1988)

VISIBILITY OF BOXES

Evidently the wood duck is not particularly skillful in locating the boxes if they are at all hidden. (McLaughlin and Grice 1952)

We suggest that if nest boxes are distributed in inconspicuous sites, local wood duck populations will more likely achieve their full reproductive potential. (Semel and Sherman 1995)

NEST PARASITISM IN NATURAL CAVITIES VERSUS BOXES

Although nest parasitism can occur under natural conditions, its frequency is apparently lower and the size of clutches is smaller than in man-made nesting situations. (Semel and Sherman 1986)

We suggest that the high parasitism rates observed in natural cavities reflect . . . that conspecific nest parasitism is pervasive among wood ducks, even in natural tree cavities that are more widely dispersed and well-hidden than nest boxes. (Roy Nielsen et al. 2006)

Readers should not place too much emphasis on any one study. Many studies do seem to contradict others, but this shouldn't be too surprising. Each study was done at a different time, in a different place or region, in different habitats, with different initial densities of wood ducks and different possible predator communities or populations, different local food resources, and different weather events. So, the lack of one true right answer to a question isn't surprising.

No one type of nest house or placement meets all the requirements imposed by the diversity of habitat and predators. Consequently, each nest house program needs to be designed with local conditions in mind. (Bellrose 1976)

Scientists conduct studies, the results of which inform and guide management. Best practices of past decades may, with subsequent research, differ from the best practices of today. How do we use this information in our own conservation efforts? First, read as much as possible to find studies as similar as possible to your situation. Talk to local experts. Most importantly, observe, watch, take notes, and watch some more. Where are the wood ducks in your area, and what are they doing there? How many wood ducks are around? Is your area similar to high-density wood duck areas yet doesn't have many woodies?

After you've put all that information together for yourself, try something. Put some nest boxes up at what you feel will be the ideal locations, placing them with densities and at heights based on what you've learned. Monitor each box over three or four years. If you have high nest success, keep doing what you're doing. And keep monitoring. If you have low success, move some boxes. And keep monitoring.

This is the basis of what biologists call adaptive management or strategic habitat conservation. Take an action. Monitor, research, and analyze the data. Learn from the data. If the original action is working, keep doing it. If it's not working, read some more, talk to more people, observe more, and do something different. And keep monitoring. Repeat until successful.

Nest boxes placed in open, parklike forests seem to be used more often than boxes in dense forests. Ryan et al. (1998) found more than 80 percent of ducklings had hatched in upland forest farther than one kilometer from permanent water, suggesting that production from upland forest has been underestimated. Robb and Bookhout (1995) determined that nests farther from water suffered less predation, primarily from raccoons, than those closer to water. They were looking at nests within 150 yards of the water, however. More generally, the farther the nest is from the water, the more vulnerable the ducklings are to predation, accidents, or obstacles along the way to reaching it (F. Leopold 1966).

In Illinois, nest parasitism was greater in floodplains than in upland forest, but the parasitism rate was not high enough to suppress production (Roy Nielsen et al. 2006). In a related study, Roy Nielsen and Gates (2007) found that predation in floodplain forests declined during floods, but that predation rates did not change over the same time period in upland forest cavities. McLaughlin and Grice (1952) found that boxes near the edges of swampy areas were most susceptible to raccoons, since raccoons were more common in these habitats.

Consider the bigger picture when placing nest boxes: Are nest boxes adding to regional or flyway populations? Put another way, do they add to the fall flight? More pragmatically, is the time and effort spent on nest boxes worth it on a regional scale?

The science is mixed. Heusmann (2000) studied nest boxes in Massachusetts and calculated that they contributed 4,300 fledged ducklings to the fall flight. In the years of that study, hunters in the state harvested 5,500 wood ducks. Nest boxes contributed almost 80 percent of the harvest. Granted, some of the ducks harvested in the state were hatched farther north, and some of the state's ducks were harvested farther south, but it's still a sizable percentage.

Soulliere (1986) did a similar study in Wisconsin and came to the opposite conclusion. He estimated that only about one-third of one percent of the state's hens nested in boxes. It would take an enormous effort by volunteers and wildlife biologists to build enough boxes to accommodate even one percent of the state's hens.

When looking at nest boxes, however, we do have to look beyond the mathematics of counting eggs across a state or region. We should also look at local populations, regional populations, and people's involvement in conservation.

Benefits accrued by people participating in such programs include a sense of doing something tangible for wildlife, and wood ducks can be highly responsive to such efforts. But what are the benefits to the wood duck population as a whole? (Hawkins et al. 1988)

Artificial "houses" for wood duck nesting are an adjunct to natural cavities. Because of the extensive nature of riverine habitats used by breeding wood ducks, natural cavities produce the vast majority of all young. . . . Nevertheless and fortunately, where more concise wetlands occur—such as marshes, swamps, beaver and farm ponds—nest houses have contributed substantially to local wood duck populations. (Bellrose et al. 1993)

The comment above brings up an interesting management issue. When scientists and wildlife managers talk about populations of waterfowl, their reference point is usually at the scale of a state, flyway, or continent. Do nest boxes substantially influence the fall flight, given the presence of nest cavities? Hard to say.

Nest boxes can add to the local population, however. For you, your family, or your hunting club or conservation organization, that local population may be just as important as the number of birds traversing the length of the flyway each fall. Neither viewpoint is right or wrong, which highlights a basic theme of this book: boxes have both a biological value for the wood duck and a social value to the people who become engaged in conservation work.

There are some practical considerations when it comes to managing a nest-box program. Checking nest boxes in late winter or early spring carrying a bag of cedar chips and a notebook can be a pleasant way to spend an afternoon. This works if the nest boxes are hung shoulder or head high. Dragging a ladder through the woods or wetlands to check boxes mounted higher than that can be miserable. Climbing ladders also requires several safety precautions.

> Try to imagine a balancing act with someone climbing an extension ladder without using their hands. Then picture that same someone with a nest box in one hand, a hammer in the other, and a mouthful of nails, ascending the ladder to a height of twenty feet and then awkwardly leaning forward while holding the nest box against the tree with his chest. Finally, visualize his outstretched arms around the nest box, attempting to hold a 16 penny nail in his left hand while swinging the hammer with his right, all the time trying to avoid hitting his thumb. . . . (Straka 2012)

If you want to involve kids, lifting them up or putting them on your shoulders to see into a nest box mounted six feet off the ground is easy and safe. Small kids and tall ladders aren't a good combination. If you check boxes alone, mounting them over land is a good idea. If you mount them over water and need to check them by boat, boating is always best done with the buddy system for safety's sake.

Before you begin a nest-box program, no matter how large or small, there are some issues to consider.

> This moderate effort clearly demonstrates the potential for attracting breeding pairs of Wood Ducks to a suburban residential area that has proper mature trees, a suitable wetland to attract pairs and support ducklings for a short time, and a certain degree of protection from predators. (Nelson 1988)

Hanging a nest box in any random place won't do much good. Hanging a box in an area with proper trees, suitable wetlands, protection from predation, a lack of natural cavities, and a commitment to clean, monitor, and maintain those boxes can and often will do good things.

After the boxes are up, they will need annual inspection, maintenance, and occasionally repair. Nest inspections are best done in late summer after the hen and ducklings have left. First, inspect the nest box to see if eggs are present. That indicates a hen nested in the box. The next question is whether the nest was successful. Eggs that are depredated often look like they've had a bite taken out of them, literally. There may also be signs of yellow yolk dripped on the outside of the shell. If the nest was abandoned or heavily parasitized, there will be unhatched eggs in the box.

A successfully hatched egg will often have a distinct cap. Inside the egg is a membrane. For a duckling, or any bird, to hatch, they must break through both this membrane and the outer shell. Knowing what to look for, anyone can check a nest box in mid-to-late summer to determine if eggs were present, and if so whether the eggs hatched or were depredated. Digging through the wood shavings and other nest litter, look for two things: membrane and egg cap. The membrane will be "thin, white, and leathery" (Strand 2002, 2005, 2007). Find each membrane and lay them out next to each other. In many cases, you can also find the egg cap. Lay the mem-

By counting membranes and egg caps, you can determine the number of eggs that successfully hatched in the nest box. *Photo courtesy of Carrol Henderson.*

branes and egg caps out on a board or on the ground and count the number of successful hatches.

Next, determine whether all the hatched eggs were wood duck eggs or if some were from a hooded merganser. Strand (2007) finds that about 10 percent of his nest boxes contain mixed broods of woodies and hoodies. Hoody eggs tend to be a little larger, rounder, and whiter than woody eggs. Perhaps the most telling difference, though, especially if the eggs have already hatched and are partially crushed, is that hoody eggs are twice as thick as woody eggs, a difference that is immediately perceptible by pinching the eggshells between your fingers.

This monitoring is best done in summer rather than the following winter or early spring. If squirrels, mice, or other wildlife take up residence in the nest box over the fall or winter, they will eat the membranes and crush the egg remnants beyond recognition. Yet another excuse to take a walk in the woods with the dog and a kid on a summer evening.

Nest boxes can be directly monitored in other ways as well. Be aware, however, that as a general rule of thumb, the less time humans spend around an active nest box the better. Human disturbance can attract predators or cause hens to abandon nests. Unless you have a strong reason to visit the nest box, it's best for the hen and ducklings if you view it from a distance. If you do need to check the nest, watch to see when the hen leaves, then check the nest quickly and quietly.

Strand (2000) reports on boxes built into the sides of barns. The dimensions of the box are actually cut out of the barn wall and the box inserted into the space. The back side of the nest box can be replaced with one-way mirrored glass and then covered with a heavy black cloth. Observers can then carefully lift the black cloth to look into the nest box. If a dark room can be built on the back side of the nest box in which an observer could sit without allowing extra light into the box, regular glass might work just as well.

Strand (2001, 2014) has also pioneered the use of cameras to monitor nest boxes. Small cameras mounted at the ends of long flexible cables are now available that can be used to monitor nests by poking the cable's tip into the nest box to count eggs or determine if the eggs have hatched. Strand has also permanently mounted cameras inside nest boxes with cable feeds back to monitors in his house. This way, he, his grandchildren, and friends who stop by can watch every minute of egg laying, incubation, hatching, and leaving the nest. Obviously, watching a hen incubating eggs isn't the most exciting television. Strand (2001) ends his article with a quote from granddaughter Kayte: "Grandpa, can we stop watching this program now?"

F. Leopold (1951), Bellrose (1953), and Breckenridge (1956) provide some of the most detailed accounts of the nesting period. Two or three days before hatching, the ducklings begin to scratch and call within the egg. The hen then begins to utter her soft *kuk kuk kuk* sounds. This allows the ducklings to learn to recognize her voice. The ducklings then use their egg tooth, a sharp hardened "tooth" at the end of the bill that will fall off a day or so after hatching, to punch against and crack the eggshell. This is called *pipping*. The duckling rotates in the egg, cracking a circle around the wide end of the egg. The end of the egg, the cap mentioned earlier, falls away when the crack has completed the circle around the egg. The ducklings quickly dry in the nest. The hen will brood the clutch of ducklings through their first night. The following morning, the hen will leave the nest as she normally does. She will return to the nest and poke her head out the entrance hole. She remains motionless, scanning the landscape for any possible dangers. She will quickly retract into the cavity or nest box if she sees danger. This may happen only once, or it could be repeated all morning. Once the coast is clear, the hen will drop down to the ground or water, or sit on a nearby tree limb, and call to the ducklings with her *kuk kuk kuk*.

> Her calls triggered a response in the young almost immediately, and they began jumping up and down in the direction of the nest entrance. We compared the continuous jumping to popping popcorn.
> (Hester and Dermid 1973)

The ducklings do not climb up to the entrance hole in any sort of orderly way. They simply jump until their claws catch hold of something. A couple of lunges gets them to the lip of the hole. Many will fall back halfway through their ascent. Other ducklings may jump up and dislodge the one above them. Still others collide in mid-air and fall back. As more ducklings escape to the outside, the interference decreases (Hester and Dermid 1973). Despite all that seeming chaos and commotion, it often takes just a few minutes for all the ducklings to exit.

Scientists are supposed to be cold-hearted, rational individuals who do not become attached to their study subjects. That demeanor can be hard to maintain when talking about ducklings. The literature makes several references to late-hatching or weak ducklings left in the nest. Jones and Leopold (1967) recorded eighty ducklings left in nest boxes over a nine-year period, while Haramis and Thompson (1985) found forty-four ducklings left in boxes over seven years. Yes, nature is red in tooth and claw, but I can think of few more heartbreaking images than day-old ducklings too weak to answer the hen's call or peeping away in the nest with no hen outside to call to them.

6 the first year

If the nest is placed immediately over the water, the young, the moment they are hatched, scramble to the mouth of the hole, launch into the air with their little wings and feet spread out, and drop into their favourite element; but whenever their birth-place is at some distance from it, the mother carries them to it one by one in her bill, holding them so as not to injure their yet tender frame.—*Audubon 1840*

She caught them in her bill by the wing or back of the neck, and landed them safely at the foot of the tree, whence afterwards she led them to the water.—*Wilson 1839*

This period, starting when the hen calls the ducklings from the nest and extending to their arrival at the water, is the most dangerous and vulnerable period in the life of a Wood Duck.—*F. Leopold 1951*

When crossing open areas, she maintains a low profile with head down and neck extended. The ducklings are immediately behind in a compact ball or strung out in a line moving at incredible speed for such tiny creatures.—*Bellrose and Holm 1994*

One of the most remarkable aspects of the lives of young wood ducks is how they exit the cavity or box. What is even more remarkable is the amount of misinformation published on this topic. Most of this misinformation relates to hens carrying day-old ducklings from the hole down to the water.

The young, when hatched, are carried down in the bill of the female, and afterwards conducted by her to the nearest water. (Chamberlain 1891)

[T]he bird flew down with the young clinging to her in some way. As she struck the water, several ducklings fell off into the stream. (Forbush 1925)

She emerged from the cavity in the stub with a young duck on her back and simply dropped straight down into the water, using her wings to check her descent. When she arrived within a foot or two of the surface, she suddenly assumed a vertical position which caused the duckling to slide from her back into the water. (Quoted in Bent 1951)

. . . while two believed that they were carried in some way between the legs. (Forbush 1925)

All of these were published by reputable ornithologists who either saw the hen themselves or heard the story from a reliable source. At least that's their story. What's most interesting is not just that the hen carries the young, but that she does it in so many different ways. No recent and reputable records describe any hen carrying any duckling. Ducklings are able to scramble to the edge of the hole, from which they fall or launch themselves into what is to them the great unknown. Some early reports describe hens helping ducklings out.

When nests are overhanging the water or close to the ground, the young are gently pushed from the nest by the mother, one by one. (Yorke 1899)

The mother started talking to her fluffy little ones and soon she began to shove them out, one by one. When the last one was out, down came the old duck . . . . (Bendick 1931)

Almost every other report, however, describes the hen calling from below or from a nearby branch. The first morning after all the ducklings have hatched, the hen will fly from the nest and land nearby, either on land or water. She will then call to the ducklings. The following excerpts imply that the ducklings simply fall or tumble from the nest, helpless victims of gravity.

[T]hey drop one by one on to the soft moss or dried leaves, their tiny bodies so enveloped in long down, scarcely harder than a leaf or feather. (Quoted in Bent 1951)

[T]hey climb to the entrance of the cavity, and like little puffballs, flutter down to the water . . . . (Roberts 1932)

. . . then tumbling out into the air and coming down gently like huge snow-flakes. They are mostly down, and why should they not fall without any danger to life or limb? (Burroughs 1905)

This is a big first step into the world, literally and figuratively. For many, that one small step is really one giant leap (for duckling kind).

Actually the little ones stood in the entrance for a moment and then took a powerful up and out jump, shooting from the box as if thrown by some invisible power. (Phillips 1925)

The first duckling at the entrance pauses for a moment before launching itself into space. With webbed feet outspread and tiny wings beating the duckling jumps without regard for the distance to the ground.
(Bellrose 1953)

This is not just a fall, but an outward jump. Often they strike the ground four to six feet out from the tree. (F. Leopold 1966)

We were surprised at the vigor the ducklings displayed in bursting forth. Twice two ducklings reached the entrance at the same time and leaped out and once three left at the same time. . . . They didn't simply drop down. They took off with a vigorous leap. . . . (Breckenridge 2009)

After all the ducklings have gathered around the hen, she will quickly take them to a safe and sheltered place in the water. This is an incredibly vulnerable time for young ducklings. In rural areas, they must look out for predators such as foxes or raccoons. In urban areas, they need to worry about feral cats and dogs. They may also encounter obstacles, natural or human-made, between them and the water. In one Iowa study, only 67 percent of ducklings from fifteen observed broods made it from the box to the water (F. Leopold 1951).

Once they get to water, the ducklings are capable of substantial movements. F. Leopold (1951) timed several broods crossing the Mississippi River from Burlington, Iowa, to Illinois at twenty minutes, a distance he estimated as three-quarters of a mile, without accounting for the current in the river. Another study estimated the top speed of a day-old duckling was a much slower six-tenths of a mile per hour (Stewart 1958).

Wood ducks travel a surprising distance in their first few weeks. One of the most common ways to track wildlife is using radio telemetry. Without it, it is often difficult to find a duck or duckling, much less to find the same individual more than once. Researchers crashing and splashing around through the habitat trying to find the birds will probably affect the birds' behaviors and locations even if they are found. For several decades, therefore, scientists have used radio telemetry to track wildlife from a distance. An animal is captured, and a small radio transmitter placed on it. Two researchers with receivers and antennas located some distance apart then triangulate on the animal and plot the animal's location on a map. Scientists can determine how far and where birds move to as well as how large their home range is. After the animals move to other locations, the researchers can go into these areas and measure the habitat where the birds were recorded without disturbing them.

Hester and Dermid (1973) report that in one study hens with young broods moved a mile and a half within eight to forty-seven hours after the ducklings left the box. Just as importantly, this study determined that a wetland with high nest-box occupancy seemed to be completely ignored by hens raising broods. All the hens who nested at this wetland moved their broods to other wetlands. In South Dakota, initial travel from nest to brood-rearing wetlands along river systems ranged from one to 2.2 miles, with a maximum of 9.6 miles (Granfors and Flake 1999). In South Carolina, broods moved up to 2.2 miles in the first day (Hepp and Hair 1977).

A brood of wood ducks does need a surprisingly large area. Hester and Dermid (1973) state that wood ducks need at least ten acres of wetland to raise a brood. Hepp and Hair (1977) found that brood home range varied from two to seventy-three acres. Webster and McGilvrey (1966), however, observed a fourteen-acre pond on which nineteen broods were reared. Even more interesting, that wetland only hatched three broods.

Hens look for both food and cover for their broods. Ducklings need to grow from weighing practically nothing, only one ounce or less (Davis et al. 2007), in early summer, to a 1.8-pound bird by early fall. That's a small amount of time to do a large amount of growing. Growth requires protein. During their first few weeks, the duckling diet is almost entirely protein-rich invertebrates. By the time they are a month old, they will have switched over to a largely vegetarian diet like their parents.

Hens and ducklings of different species can look surprisingly similar from a distance, especially if they are darting for cover. Determining the age of a brood can be similarly challenging. In wood ducks, day-old ducklings have a well-defined stripe from the eye to the back of the head, a dark glossy pattern color with a "sulphury" yellow base, and a long fan-like black tail (Nelson 1993). The following table, adapted from Bellrose and Holm (1994), helps in identifying the age of broods in the field.

Dries (1954) provides the following information to help age broods by their behavior.

UNDER 1 WEEK. In compact group at hen's side; run or swim into cover as a group when pursued; hidden in dense cover on land most of the day.

WEEKS 2-3. In close proximity of the adult hen; scatter somewhat and swim into cover when pursued; dive and swim under water for short distances.

WEEKS 4-5. Stray short distances from hen while feeding (15 feet); dive and come out on shore when pursued; rest on logs and stumps in or near water.

WEEKS 6-7. Scatter up to 50 feet while feeding; fly short distance when pursued; dive and come out on land after alighting on water; rest on stumps 2 to 4 feet above water.

WEEK 8+. Scatter widely when feeding (50+ feet); fly from sight when pursued; fly about as a family unit and frequently alight in trees.

Table 1. Feather and size characteristics for aging ducklings.

Age (days)	Plumage	Proportion of length to an adult hen	Proportion of weight of adult
1 to 6	black-brown down on crown, back and tail; sulphur on cheeks and breast	20	7
7 to 20	more brownish above; grayish below	40	15
18 to 24	scapular and tail feathers grow rapidly	45	30
25 to 30	contour feathers develop on sides	50	40
31 to 36	contour feathers develop on chest; wing coverts complete; sheaths of flight feathers appear	60	
37 to 47	contour feathers on head; colors on head appear in males; sheaths of flight feathers half-grown	75	60
48 to 60	juvenile plumage complete except for some down feathers on back; able to fly	90	90

One favorite food of young ducks is duckweed. Duckweed coats the surface of many ponds and creeks in the summer. The duckweed obviously contributes to a vegetable diet, but scores of species of invertebrates live in these duckweed mats as well. As ducklings scoop up duckweed, they also eat numerous invertebrates.

(*Facing page*) As ducks move through duckweed, they leave characteristic paths through the green mat. *Photo courtesy of Carrol Henderson.*

Ducklings also need protection from the weather and from predators. Cold nights, thunderstorms that soak their downy feathers, and other inclement weather probably take their toll on young ducklings. Even without precipitation, Davis et al. (2007) determined that cold nights reduced duckling survival. And ducklings face a whole new set of predators. Those who look upon ducklings as merely a snack include snapping turtles, bass and pike, bullfrogs, alligators, snakes, crows, herons, gulls, hawks, owls, raccoons, foxes, weasels, mink, bobcat, otter, and feral cats and dogs (McGilvrey 1969; Davis et al. 2009). As they move around in their habitat, staying out of sight in dense, thick cover is a good idea. Although lots of wildlife will eat ducklings in the water, life may be even riskier when they have to travel overland from one wetland to another. Ball et al. (1975) found that duck broods that traveled longer distances over land had greater mortality. Those first weeks when ducklings are least able to thermoregulate and escape predators are the most critical for survival. McGilvrey (1969) found that in Maryland 90 percent of duckling mortality occurred in the first two weeks. Ball et al. (1975) found similar results in Minnesota.

A review of the literature shows just how rough life as a wood duck can be. My survey of thirteen studies found an average nest parasitism rate of 51 percent. Predation destroyed 45 percent of nests. Moving from the nest box to the water accounted for 33 percent mortality. Only 51 percent of ducklings made it through their first summer, and only 46 percent of adults survived from one year to the next. Life is tough when you're a duck, at any and every stage of development. As an example, Wolfe (1989) reports that he marked thirty-one hens near Erskine, Minnesota, in 1985. In 1986, his team recaptured thirteen of the thirty-one. In the following two years, they recaptured seven and then four hens. In 1989, hen number 946-98303 was the only one of the original thirty-one remaining. Obviously, some of the hens may have nested in a different area or avoided recapture. But this study shows that even in a good year, about 50 percent of adults survive to the next year. Not a lot of old wood ducks are out there.

These numbers illustrate several principles. First, they explain why ducks lay so many eggs. As a thought exercise, imagine six pairs (twelve adults) each lay a dozen eggs. If five of those six nests are destroyed, twelve ducklings will still be hatched, essentially replacing the adult population. Ducks can handle significant levels of nest destruction and predation and still maintain their populations.

Second, the numbers show that wildlife can have a high potential rate of population growth when everything goes well. If those six nests are successful and survival is 100 percent, there would be eighty-four ducks the following year (twelve adults and seventy-two of last year's ducklings). That would be forty-two pairs of wood ducks, and each pair could lay a dozen eggs. Obviously, that's an idealized situation, but it does show that population growth can be rapid in some circumstances.

Ducks and ducklings face different levels of mortality from different sources at different points in their lives. If we can determine the key factors and key times favoring survival, we can take specific management actions to grow the population.

7 habitat and migration

Acre for acre, few wetlands surpass the quality of a beaver pond as wood duck habitat.
—*Bateman 1977*

[R]educed parasitism and increased hatchability occur when artificial nesting structures
are placed in habitats and at densities resembling the natural circumstances in which
Wood Ducks evolved.—*Semel et al. 1988*

By the time most woodies have begun their northward migration in February, some already
have started nesting in the Deep South.—*Bellrose et al. 1993*

Wood Duck populations growth since the early 1900s paralleled expansion and maturation
of deciduous forests across the region.—*Soulliere et al. 2017*

There is a discrepancy in the wood duck literature when it comes to habitat. Some writers talk about how secluded and hard to reach wood duck
habitat is.

Its favorite haunts are small lakes, weedy ponds, or shady streams . . . .
(Fisher 1901)

He much prefers the woods to open waters, and is found, for the most part,
on small wooded rivers and creeks clothed with timber, and ponds snug in
the forest. (Askins 1931)

. . . secluded inland pools and streams bordered by woods and forest
swamps. (Kortright 1943)

Note how intimate and closed in these writers make the habitat sound,
with words such as "haunts," "snug," and "secluded." Others explicitly
state that wood duck habitat and human habitat are distinctly different.

In summer, they may be found about the edges of clear ponds and lakes, especially those located in woods remote from human habitation. (Reed 1936)

Others, however, write that the wood duck readily accepts the presence of people.

Recently, however, increasing numbers have deserted the lowlands and have actually penetrated to the very hearts of our river towns where they have nested in holes in the trees along the streets, showing favoritism to sites in parks, cemeteries, and courtyards. (Musselman 1948)

In spring the birds will nest in apple trees, or large elms and maples, near houses, or wherever big old trees exist. . . . (Ripley 1957)

Moreover, they occur almost everywhere, in small creeks and large rivers, farm ponds and lakes, marshes, and swamps. They are indigenous to wooded bottomlands and impenetrable swamps, but they will nest in towns. (Benson and Bellrose 1964)

In some cases, they blend in with the scenery of the rural farmstead.

They have been so far domesticated as to run about at large in the barn-yard like ordinary fowls. (Chamberlain 1891)

It is not seclusive, often making its abode near towns, perhaps in the vicinity of farmhouses, where it may be found feeding or associating with barn-yard ducks. (Fisher 1901)

On the outskirts of villages these ducks often fearlessly enter the barnyard to pick up the poultry's grain. (Blanchan 1905)

We can over-exaggerate the idea that wood ducks *prefer* to nest near people because we see so many of them nesting near us, both in natural cavities and in boxes. Italics below are added.

In fact, *most of them were found* within a short distance of occupied buildings. Nests were found in trees directly beside village walks and alongside of cottages. In one village 4 nests were occupied within the court house yard. (Gigstead 1938)

Most of the nesting occurs in natural cavities found in mature trees *out of sight from most people*. But where natural cavities are in short supply, Wood Ducks readily accept man-made structures as nesting places, often in one's backyard. (Hawkins 1986)

Hawkins (1986) states that cavities are hard for people to find. Gigstead (1938) says that nests, whether in cavities or boxes, were found by people where people generally are. People find nests in town or on farmsteads because that's where people are. Very few people are out walking through the knee-deep muck, crawling over downed tree trunks, and navigating other hazards that often characterize floodplain forests. Also, natural cavities can be well hidden, and we may walk right past them even in the easiest-to-walk-through forests. Wood ducks don't necessarily prefer to nest near people, but when they do nest near people, they are more likely to be seen.

As described earlier, wood ducks depend somewhat on pileated (and formerly on ivory-billed) woodpeckers to create nesting cavities. In the late 1800s and early 1900s, beaver populations were also shrinking due to a legacy of overtrapping. Beavers dam small forested streams, backing up water into the forests and creating wetlands. These forested wetlands make nearly ideal wood duck habitat.

A large beaver pond usually is ideal wood duck habitat and is especially suited to rearing young. (Hester and Dermid 1973)

In Alabama, beaver ponds probably come closest to meeting all the life requirements of wood ducks. (Beshears 1974)

In many cases, the dam backs water up over the roots of the trees, killing some of them. This makes it even easier for woodpeckers to excavate holes in those trees for themselves and eventually for woodies. Young ducklings could leap from the holes in the dead trees straight into the beaver pond.

This brings up two questions. How many beavers were there? What impact did beavers have on the regional landscape? Biologists have asked and argued over these questions for the last hundred plus years. A similar question is asked about the number of bison on the prairies or the number of passenger pigeons in eastern North America. These primarily thought exercises can be intellectually stimulating, but in the end every number is a guess, no matter how well-informed or how well supported by anecdotal evidence and mathematical extrapolation.

Seton (1929) was one of the first to try to estimate the continental beaver population before Europeans arrived. He cites Radford, who set the beaver population in the Adirondack Mountains of New York at one million, or sixty to the square mile. Extrapolate those numbers across the North American continent, and Seton concludes that the population could have been as high as 400,000,000. Palmer, cited in Seton, estimated the beaver population in Algonquin Park, Ontario, at 100,000, or fifty per square mile. Seton goes on to make a conservative estimate that there were at least 60,000,000 beavers in North America. He later states that twenty beavers to the square mile is not an overestimate in beaver country.

Seton cites Morgan's early journals, written near Marquette, Michigan, in which he notes surveying sixty-three beaver dams in an area six-by-eight miles. Morgan states that he may have recorded only half the number of dams and lodges that were actually there. Burchsted et al. (2010) estimated that some areas have dams as frequently as every sixty yards of creek or stream. Today, beaver ponds occupy as much as 15 percent of all the land in northern Minnesota (Johnston and Naiman 1990). We can never know exactly how many beavers lived there before overtrapping reduced the populations in the early to mid 1800s. We do know that whatever beavers there were would have profoundly affected the local forests, rivers, creeks, streams, wetlands, and hydrology over large areas. What effect did beavers have on the regional landscape? Millions of beavers would build a lot of dams in forested parts of the country, reaching to practically everywhere wood ducks would have nested. Removing all those beavers from the landscape would have dramatically affected wetlands, and therefore wood ducks, in many areas.

Beaver dams and the wetlands they create make ideal wood duck habitat for several reasons. First, almost by definition, beaver dams are in wooded areas or areas with trees nearby, putting beaver-created wetlands next to or in forests. Second, beaver dams usually occur in stream or river networks. A hen wood duck and her brood would simply need to go upstream or downstream over a dam or two to find more or better habitat (Hepp and Hair 1977).

Because the wetlands beavers create are so important to so many different species of wildlife—furry, feathery, scaly, or slimy—many conservationists and scientists refer to beavers as ecosystem engineers. Another term often used for beavers is keystone species. Beaver activity affects dozens of other species.

Beavers and their dams also provide a number of ecosystem services for people. Dams hold back floodwater during periods of heavy rain. Dams collect sediment from upstream erosion. By holding water in the watershed instead of letting it flow too quickly downstream, the dam causes water to sink down into the soil, recharging groundwater. A watershed or drainage with and without beavers will vary greatly and will have differing levels of abundance and wildlife diversity.

This brings us back to wood ducks. Imagine the eastern forest in the 1500s. Mature trees and woodpeckers were abundant. Beavers, their dams, and ponds backed up by these dams were also common. This would have created ideal brood-rearing cover in the spring and early summer as well as roosting areas throughout the rest of the year over much of the eastern half of the country.

Today, with beavers recovered to pest status in many areas, a sagging lumber industry that doesn't harvest as many trees as it once did in many areas, and continued growth in woodpecker populations, wood ducks have it better than they've had it in the last hundred years. This adds a new element to the conservation story relative to previous decades. The following quotes span more than a century.

> Its tree-loving habit is one of the causes of decrease. . . . In many localities where the Wood Duck was known to breed until within a few years, it is not now found, owing to the fact that every tree suitable for nesting has been cut down. (Dutcher 1907)

> The wood duck depends on natural cavities for nesting; and since much of Massachusetts is in second growth hardwoods and abandoned farm lands, providing additional nesting places appeared to be a logical management practice. (McLaughlin and Grice 1952)

> Although the density of suitable wood duck nest cavities was not high, cavities are nevertheless abundant because large areas of forest are available for wood duck nesting. Numbers of cavities should increase as Wisconsin's second growth forests continue to mature. (Soulliere 1988)

> Because current and future estimates indicate sufficient nest sites to support growing cavity-nesting duck populations in the north central United States, we recommend regional management efforts focus on protecting, restoring, and maintaining quality wetlands in proximity to hardwood. (Denton et al. 2012)

Due to maturing forests in many parts of the wood duck range, natural tree cavities may no longer be the limiting factor they were in the past. Denton et al. (2012) estimated that there were 13.2 million suitable cavity trees near water from Minnesota to Missouri to Ohio.

That said, hollow, diseased, or dead trees are of little value to foresters. In many cases, forests are managed for healthy, disease- and rot-free trees that can eventually be turned into nice straight boards at the sawmill. Often these diseased, crooked, twisted, or damaged trees, the trees most valuable to many species of wildlife, are cut down to provide more light and more room for the straight healthy trees. This is exactly what A. Leopold wrote about in "A Mighty Fortress."

Forestry practices, such as culling wolf or deformed trees and girdling or poisoning species of no economic value, have further reduced the environment for wood ducks. (Sincock et al. 1964)

Wildlife managers will have a greater impact on wood ducks by advising on forestry operations, rather than actively providing nest sites.
(Soulliere 1988)

At other times, foresters may wish to harvest trees before they get so large that they develop heart rot and are largely unusable. This can be especially critical in northern areas where aspen is needed by wood ducks, buffleheads, and goldeneyes. Aspen are often cut on a shorter rotation that doesn't allow for large trees, let alone large trees with some rot and eventual cavities. Given these circumstances, working with forestry agencies and the timber industry may be more effective for regional wood duck populations than building and maintaining nest boxes.

In my previous book, *Sky Dance*, I describe the problem facing many wildlife species from golden-winged warblers to woodcock to lynx to moose: lack of young or early successional forest. To oversimplify, the greater the timber harvest, the better for these species. For the wood duck, however, it could be argued that the exact opposite is true. Oversimplifying again, the less timber harvested, the better for wood ducks and other species with similar needs. Any management action will affect almost every species. What is detrimental to some species is beneficial to others. This idea recalls our earlier discussion of predators. Altering the habitat to favor wood ducks over predators will be far more effective in the long run than trapping raccoons.

This is where wildlife biologists and foresters can work together to develop an overall landscape management plan that doesn't leave and doesn't take too many trees in the wrong places. A mix and a diversity of tree species, tree age classes, and forest structure is needed across the regional landscape. Given a good mix of habitats, every species of wildlife will find nearly ideal habitat somewhere on the landscape.

One issue that foresters are looking into is the decline of oaks across the eastern half of North America (Abrams 1992, 2003). Oaks, especially white oaks, are more fire tolerant than species such as ash, maple, and beech. With a decline in prescribed fires in the eastern part of the country, oak forests are being replaced by forests dominated by maples and other tree species. Yes, maple, beech, and ash can provide some soft mast for wood ducks and other wildlife. But given the affinity between wood ducks and acorns, this long-term decline in oaks across the wood duck range could have long-term effects on wood duck populations.

Prescribed fire is generally treated as an ecological disturbance, and disturbances are usually associated with early successional or younger forests. In this case, however, we may need an ecological disturbance to maintain mature oak trees in our forests.

To protect wood ducks, we also need to look specifically at the wetlands they most prefer. Wood ducks don't necessarily like the big open waters that many people like for boating and other activities. Wood duck wetlands are messy.

> Suitable wood duck brood habitat, in general terms, seems to consist of a patchy pattern of emergent cover interlaced with a network of open water passageways. (Webster and McGilvrey 1966)

> Composition and interspersion of cover is more important to wood ducks than any other species of waterfowl. They require close cover to feel secure, both around them and overhead, but which allows free movement through the water. (Beshears 1974)

The recipe seems to be some open water, some submergent vegetation, some emergent vegetation (cattails and bulrushes), some brush, and overhead cover to hide under. Fuller (1975) recommends 50:50 vegetation to

(*Facing page*) The large mature trees in this photo along the edge of this wetland are oaks. Almost all the saplings in this area are maples. It's not difficult to imagine what this forest will look like when all the oaks die.

open water for breeding habitat and 75:25 vegetation to open water for brood-rearing habitat. McGilvrey (1969) breaks this down further into 25 percent water, 30 percent shrubs, 40 percent emergent vegetation, and 5 percent trees. Thompson and Baldassarre (1989) found that wood ducks prefer wooded wetlands in late summer and fall and wooded swamps in late fall. Parr et al. (1979) determined that wood ducks prefer buttonbush swamps over flooded timber. Several studies identified significant overland movements or long distances along streams and rivers between nest-box locations to brood-raising habitat. If managers can identify these productive wetlands and place nest boxes in these areas, travel time and resulting mortality could be diminished (Davis et al. 2009).

This is where habitat studies can become confusing. What are the exact definitions of wooded wetland, wooded swamp, buttonbush swamp, and flooded timber? They all sound fairly similar. No one universal definition of any given habitat has been established, nor do habitats usually fit within an ideal classification system. Wildlife managers sometimes perform an exercise in which they review a set of habitat descriptions and then visit a series of sites in different habitats. Each manager or researcher classifies each site, and they then compare their results at the end of the day. Often, opinions on how to classify many of the sites differ widely.

Davis et al. (2007) identified shrub-scrub habitats in two different study areas. In one area, 58 percent of ducklings survived, while in the other, classified in the same way, only 21 percent of ducklings survived. Clearly, something in the two habitats that the scientists cannot detect affects the ducks differently. Or perhaps the predator community in one area is greater than in the other. Or was the summer weather in one less favorable to ducklings?

Wood duck habitats range from open water to marsh to swamp to forest. Marsh, swamp, and forest will consist of different structures of vegetation, different densities of vegetation, and different species of trees and other plants. The lines we draw separating or classifying these habitats can often be somewhat arbitrary. This site is mostly forested but a little swampy. That site is primarily marsh but has some swamp characteristics. Mother Nature doesn't like to be pigeonholed into some statistically derived human-made classification scheme.

One key to wood duck habitat, especially as it relates to the habitat's "messy" look, is that ducks need someplace to get out of the water. These areas provide safe places for young ducklings to dry off and warm up and for adults to loaf or preen. These can include muskrat mounds, beaver lodges, or downed timber floating on the surface.

> Open water is interspersed with vegetation. Runs penetrate the shrub thickets, providing avenues of movement and escape with screening branches overhead. Logs and exposed bars, used as loafing and preening sites, are scattered about, and flooded trees provide cover . . . .
> (Hester and Dermid 1973)

> Ideal brood habitat for wood ducks is a shallow, marshy area, full of fallen logs and dense overhanging shrubs and trees. (Bateman 1977)

Cottrell et al. (1988) found that wooded shoreline, fallen trees, and aquatic vegetation were the three factors that best explained suitable wood duck brood habitat. Beard (1964) suggests that loafing areas such as downed logs could be a limiting factor for wood duck habitat. Wood duck habitat is not speedboat country. In fact, it may be difficult to navigate in a canoe or kayak.

In some cases, habitat can almost seem to interfere with habitat. This simply shows that wood ducks, waterfowl, and all wildlife need different resources at different times of the year.

> American lotus was a preferred habitat during much of the postbreeding period, but becomes unavailable in late fall, has little value as a waterfowl food, and often inhibits growth of valuable food plants. . . . These conflicting aspects of American lotus should be considered within the context of the wetland complex before implementing management and propagation practices. (Thompson and Baldassarre 1989)

Is American lotus good or bad? Yes and no: It depends on the situation. This again points to the importance of habitat diversity. An area with zero

Wood duck habitat is messy, with dead trees, muskrat houses, or brush piles in the water and a diversity of vegetation structures and plant species.

lotus would provide little cover. An area with 100 percent lotus would provide little food. A patchy habitat with some lotus here but not there provides both food and cover.

Working in North Carolina, Fuller (1975) lists "important species" of trees for wood ducks as sycamore, American beech, elm, red maple, tupelo, sweet gum, and bald cypress. In Alabama, Beshears (1974) lists sycamore, beech, ash, birch, box elder, elm, hickory, and maple as "unimportant." How can sycamore, beech, and maple be both important and unimportant? Are North

Carolina and Alabama that different? The answer is another question: Important for what? Fuller is discussing trees with cavities for nesting, while Beshears is discussing mast production for food. Statements on habitat need to be taken in context when discussing whether a species is deemed desirable or undesirable and for what wildlife.

When it comes to habitat, scientists and managers are often better botanists than are the resident wildlife species. We tend to obsess about the trees, grasses, and wildflowers we manage for or plant. While this is important when it comes to oaks, wild rice, duckweed, and a few other key food plants, wildlife are probably far more interested in the structure of the vegetation than in the species of tree. Descriptions of habitat, north, south, and in between, are pretty similar structurally. Aspen is scarce in Louisiana, as is bald cypress in New England. Show botanists photos of habitats in different states, and they would see quite different habitats. Show architects photos of habitats in different states, and they see habitats that look quite similar.

A consistent trait of wood duck habitat and behavior is the use of roost ponds. These ponds are used year after year by wood ducks in what seems to be a relatively permanent feature of wood duck behavior, a trait Bellrose and Holm (1994) describe as "seldom seen in other waterfowl." Wood ducks congregate on these ponds, in some cases in the thousands, even though other suitable wetlands are nearby. Bellrose and Holm (1994) surveyed the literature on the habitat wood ducks require in these ponds and came up with descriptions such as "small areas of open water . . . dense woody and/or herbaceous emergent vegetation . . . dense stands of buttonbrush . . . wooded swamps . . . shrub swamps . . . buttonbrush fringed backwater lakes and wetlands supporting a mixture of buttonbush and black willow." Thompson and Baldassarre (1989) found that the presence of American lotus was an important factor in identifying night roosts because it provides "extremely dense overhead cover."

It's not entirely clear what the function of roost ponds is for wood ducks or the function of roosting among birds in general. It may be a way for unpaired males or males after the breeding season to congregate in late spring or early summer. In late summer, roosting may allow adults and juveniles to congregate and juveniles to learn about the local habitat from the adults. Juvenile wood ducks can follow adults from the roost ponds to the best feeding locations in the area, which they may have had trouble finding by themselves. Parr et al. (1979) found that wood ducks tend to stay within about 1.4 miles of the roost ponds. Finally, in the fall, the ponds may aid hens and drakes in pairing. These roost areas may serve as a focal point for wood ducks within a regional habitat complex. Thompson and Baldassarre (1989) found that identifying and protecting these roost ponds was essential to maintaining an overall complex of wetland habitats for postbreeding ducks.

One popular management technique for lowland habitat for species like mallards and wood ducks is the greentree reservoir. These are more commonly used in the South than the North. Managers flood oak-dominated forests for a few months each winter. Water depth is usually no more than fifteen-to-eighteen inches so that dabbling ducks can tip up and eat acorns off the forest floor at the bottom of the reservoir. This management method often requires a dike to hold the water, a large number of oak trees, the right soils (sandy soils won't hold water), and a source of water. In some cases, water from an adjacent creek or stream can be diverted into the reservoir. In other cases, water is pumped into the reservoir. In the late winter, the manager opens gates to release the water. As long as the water floods the trees while they are dormant in the winter and not actively growing in the summer, this technique does not appear to damage the forest. That said, the general recommendation is to leave the area dry every third or fourth winter. Thompson and Baldassarre (1989) and Drobney and Frederickson (1979) recommend flooding an area slowly, allowing wood ducks foraging on acorns to follow the edge of the water as it gradually moves into the forest.

This seems like an awful lot of work that may use an awful lot of fossil fuel, and it can be. Many will argue that nature should be left natural, without all this interference. That's a very valid point. Others argue that many floodplain forests are over-engineered ecosystems, which require engineering—also a valid point in some cases and places. Writing about the Crystal Lake Hunt Club on the east side of the Mississippi River, Frederic Leopold (1984) notes that "during times of flood Crystal Lake was a flowing part of the Mississippi River." Describing the amount of engineering that has gone into the river, specifically the size and height of the dikes that now separate the Mississippi River from Crystal Lake, Krohne (2008) writes, "You look *up* at barges passing by in the Mississippi." Are greentree reservoirs that pump water on and off a site forms of management that are too manipulative, or do they use reasonable engineering processes to compensate for other engineering to restore a semblance of floodplain dynamics? In wildlife management, the easiest questions become ever more complicated the closer you look.

* * * *

It seems to be an American trait that we like to buy our property "out in nature" and then spend the next couple of decades making it look like the suburban lawn we just left. It often drives wildlife managers crazy to see lakeside homeowners clearing away all vegetation. It makes the wildlife even madder. People plant turf grass down to the edge of the water, mow it frequently, and add fertilizers that quickly wash off the lawn and into the lake, causing algal blooms. Then they add unsightly riprap along the edge of the water as protection against erosion that the vegetation they just cleared away had provided naturally.

Bradley (1994, 2005) provides some guidelines for managing wood duck wetlands. Not everyone can apply all of his suggestions but implementing the ones you can will benefit wildlife. First, keep fallen logs and brush in the water. If possible, pile brush over the ice in the winter. With melt, it will sink into the wetland. Brush can be created by trimming shrubs and tree branches. Woodies like to sit on horizontal tree limbs. Where practical and safe, trim tree branches to maximize the number of horizontal limbs.

Fell trees along the edge of the wetland, especially multitrunked trees that can survive if one trunk is cut. If possible, don't cut the log completely free from the stump but keep the trunk hinged to the stump. This will allow the tree to continue to leaf out for at least a couple more years. Piles of weeds or hay bales placed on the water's edge make a good substitute muskrat house. Each of these strategies will create areas where adults can preen and ducklings can get out of the water to warm themselves on cold days. They can also provide overhead protection from weather or aerial predators. Last, they will provide a diversity of habitats for the aquatic insects on which hens and ducklings depend for egg production and growth.

Beavers, as noted, create ideal habitat for wood ducks. By felling trees and piling brush, landowners essentially mimic the wood ducks' best friend. Put another way, don't make the wetland or shoreline look clean and neat and tidy. The messier and more heterogeneous it looks, the more the ducks will use it. And this is where human and wildlife views of the world can differ. A few paragraphs earlier I stated that riprap was unsightly. That was my opinion, but every wood duck would agree with me.

Given the amount of white rock lining the shorelines of lakeside homes, many people disagree with this characterization. These homeowners would find unsightly the downed trees, brush piles, "weeds," and other debris that wildlife prefer. Neither opinion is absolutely right or wrong. We can, however, say that our actions as landowners do impact habitat and wildlife. We can't have it both ways. If we want to watch abundant wildlife out our windows, we may need to leave things a little messier than the suburban esthetic often favors.

Before doing any work on any wetland, check with your local regulatory agency or state or federal wildlife agency. Laws and restrictions in many areas identify what a person can and can't do with wetlands.

* * * *

(*Facing page*) Felling trees into the water for adults and ducklings to use to dry off, warm up, and preen simply simulates the activities of beavers.

Especially in the North, wood duck habitat is really only good for part of the year. The rest of the year everything is frozen. In the fall, northern wood ducks have to move south to find suitable habitat to survive the winter months. This of course raises the question, why do the ducks move north in the spring? If the south is so great, why don't they just stay there all year long?

This introduces the mysteries of migration. Note the use of the plural "mysteries" when referencing migration. There are dozens of ways to migrate and scores of reasons to migrate, and most scientists agree that we understand very few of the ways or the reasons. Actually, the *why* questions are much more difficult than the *how* questions.

It's pretty easy to say that birds fly to northern habitats in the spring and to southern habitats in the fall. That's true in most of North America for most species. In other parts of the world, that's not how it works at all. Some species migrate up and down mountains, some migrate east to west, some migrate more in some years than in others, and some species don't migrate at all. Finding one ecological principle to explain all that variation and all those strategies has stymied researchers for centuries. Dingle (1996) states that "perhaps no other behavior has suffered so much from confusion of definition as migration."

It's hard to miss the wood duck migration in the spring. To the eye or ear, they are hardly inconspicuous. Although they leave the North relatively early in the fall, presumably avoiding any threat of cold autumn weather, they are also one of the first ducks to return in the spring. In my home in central Minnesota, wood ducks are often the first duck I see in the spring, usually beating mallards by a day or two. In the last two years, they have shown up on March 21 and 23. And when they come, they come in force.

Arriving simultaneously with the other earlier species, none other braves the last rigors of the departing winter in the closing days of the Minnesota March with greater spirit. And when they come, like the rains of the tropics, they pour in until every pool in the woodlands has been deluged with them. (Hatch 1892)

And what better bird could there be to bring color and cheer to the gloomy mud, dirty snow and slush, and overcast skies of late winter or early spring in the northland?

Wood ducks conduct what is called partial migration. Some birds migrate and some don't. Birds born in Minnesota may only migrate south to Missouri or may continue to Louisiana. Birds born in Missouri may winter in Louisiana. Some birds born in Arkansas or Louisiana may be year-round residents and not migrate at all.

The southward migration amounts to no more than withdrawal from the northern half of the summer range. (Cooke 1906)

How do we explain these differences? Partly it's genetic. Earlier chapters described how well female wood ducks can navigate back to the area where they were born and raised, often very precisely. So one reason wood ducks migrate northward is because their parents and grandparents did.

Another reason is because the North has some limiting resources the birds are able to exploit. Migration is incredibly risky. Birds fly thousands of miles not knowing what they'll find along the way for stopover sites and not being exactly sure of what they'll find when they get where they are going. This behavior can only evolve if the costs of migration are less than the benefits. Kerlinger (1995) states that the "foundation of all explanations is food" when determining why a species migrates. With wood ducks, we could add nest cavities as a limiting resource. Many wood ducks will winter in the Gulf Coast states. Imagine the competition that would occur for food and cavities if all wood ducks bred in those states. The hen not only has to think about food resources for herself, but also for her ducklings.

Staying put has its advantages. Some southern wood ducks begin nesting as early as February (Hester and Dermid 1973), and they are often able to raise multiple broods in one year. They also avoid the stresses and uncertainties of migration. But with migration, birds can spread out across the northern United States and southern Canadian provinces. This allows them to exploit millions of potential nesting cavities as well as new food resources. For these birds, the costs of migration are less than the benefits provided by all these resources.

One of the greatest puzzles of migration is navigation. Birds don't just fly north in the spring. They don't just fly to some general area. Many wood ducks and other birds fly back to the exact same place, even the same nest box, as last year. What cues do they use to navigate so precisely? We don't know. They may use the sun's position, the stars, the polarization of sunlight through the atmosphere, landmarks, olfaction (smell), magnetism, or some other cue scientists don't recognize. More likely, birds use some combination of these methods.

From a discussion about habitat, migration, and changing habitats throughout the migration season, we can more directly discuss habitat management. Two basic mindsets apply when managing habitat, with lots of variation in and between the two. Neither is right or wrong; they just represent philosophical differences. One mindset says that we can manipulate, manage, and engineer habitat to create the best habitat to directly benefit a particular species. The other mindset says that if we create diverse and resilient habitat, wildlife living there will take care of themselves.

Many sources in the literature state that water should be managed to achieve depths of three-to-eighteen inches, the maximum a dabbling duck can dabble. One way to interpret or misinterpret that statement is to manage everything for eighteen inches as the best depth. That's fine for a normal weather year, whatever normal weather is. But what about drought years? What about flood periods? If everything is managed for a narrow range of conditions, a drought will leave us with no habitat. The same can be said for flooding.

Some read the dietary literature for a specific area and see that the writers state that wood ducks in those areas prefer pin oaks. This might encourage people to plant and manage only for pin oaks. That's fine, except that pin oaks, like most oaks, have mast years. The mast years will be really good, but the non-mast years could be really bad. Planting several species of native oaks appropriate to the habitats and soils provides a bit of an insurance policy for years when the pin oaks don't produce many acorns.

In recent decades, perspectives have begun to shift from the perhaps oversimplified narrative that wood ducks need us to build them nest boxes.

> Managers must identify potential limiting factors so that conservation efforts can be focused where they are most likely to provide benefits.
> (Roy Nielsen et al. 2007)

If nest sites aren't the limiting factor, however, we can build all the nest boxes we want and we won't change the population at all. "Build a nest box" is an easy narrative to sell. Today's story is a little more complicated.

> Although forest age structure and nest cavity abundance continue to increase, wood duck populations may have stabilized in recent years. . . . Reasons for the apparent leveling of population growth are uncertain, though presence of invertebrate-rich wetlands available during the breeding period has been identified as a possible limitation. (Soulliere et al. 2017)

> We suggest that providing a diversity of habitat types will increase the probability of meeting the needs of breeding females throughout the breeding season, especially in areas where wetland conditions frequently change.
> (Hartke and Hepp 2004)

Note that Soulliere and colleagues don't just say "wetlands"; they say "invertebrate-rich wetlands." Wetlands are more than just a hole in the ground full of water. Hartke and Hepp bring up that word again: *diversity.* Wood ducks need areas with different oaks as well as other tree species. They need different forms of aquatic vegetation. They need a range of wetlands of different sizes and different depths and at different places on the landscape. The phrase "where wetlands frequently change" can be applied almost anywhere, since wetlands and rivers are some of the most dynamic ecosystems in the world.

The old narrative, stated or implied, is that wood ducks need a small pond and a nest box. The new narrative is that natural cavities may be abundant. Wood duck hens and broods cover large areas and visit many wetlands. Wetland quality, invertebrate abundance, and vegetation structure are all very important. The wood duck diet changes seasonally and in some cases weekly. Diversity is important at every level. Hens need a diversity of invertebrates to meet their nutritional needs while laying eggs. Structural diversity in wetlands is important. Diversity of oaks and other mast-producing trees is important. The diversity of trees in the forests where wood ducks nest is important. Diversity of habitats provides an insurance policy against annual and seasonal fluctuations in weather and climate. The new narrative is really complicated.

Adding and maintaining a few hundred nest boxes, a large undertaking, would have very little impact on regional wood duck populations. That is not to say that a wood duck nest-box program shouldn't be used to boost local production, but with limited time and budgets, nest boxes might not make the best use of conservation resources in some areas. Today more than ever, we have to do conservation smarter and better than we have in the past, relying on science to inform our decisions. If nest boxes won't increase wood duck populations, conservation efforts should probably focus on other activities, such as wetland restoration.

Tree cavity abundance will likely continue to increase naturally with present forestry practices. Cooperation with foresters and commercial contractors can maximize future cavity production. In areas like Wisconsin, wood duck management should be redirected from actively supplying nest sites to enhancing more critical life requisites. (Soulliere 1988)

Our results suggest that availability of nest and den sites for cavity-dependent wildlife will increase as eastern deciduous forests mature over

the next half century. Cost-effectiveness of artificial nest-box programs should be reevaluated in light of projected changes in tree cavity availability as deciduous forests mature in the eastern United States.
(Roy Nielsen et al. 2007)

We don't manage wildlife, we manage habitat. The habitat takes care of the wildlife. Aldo Leopold (1942) wrote that "the objective is to teach the student to see the land, to understand what he sees, and enjoy what he understands. I say land rather than wildlife, because wildlife cannot be understood without understanding the landscape as a whole." Like any species of wildlife, managing wood ducks requires us to look at the big picture: what wood ducks eat, what eats wood ducks, where they live, how much they move and over how large an area, and the temporal and spatial patterns of their migration.

8 hunting then and now

They are not uncommon in the markets of the Eastern and Middle States, and are justly esteemed as food.—*Chamberlain 1891*

At the present it may be killed at any time and gunners often begin shooting the young birds in June, when they are not more than two-thirds grown.—*A. H. Howell 1911*

Spring shooting which went on merrily even after the ducks had laid their eggs brought the species nearly to extinction in the early part of the twentieth century.—*Forbush 1925*

He recalls a fall about 1883 when he killed over a thousand ducks. . . . Wood ducks were then the most abundant duck, he says, with mallards a close second.—*Hawkins 1940*

As described in the first chapter, wood ducks were so scarce in the early 1900s that they were one of the few birds specifically identified in the Migratory Bird Treaty. They were scarce and getting scarcer.

It is only necessary to point to the fact that this handsome bird is now almost unknown in many places where once it was common. . . . (Fisher 1901)

Our chief game warden, Mr. J. C. Porterfield, says that in his boyhood home in the western part of the state [Ohio] Wood Ducks flying to and from their nests were one of the most familiar sights, comparable to Robins and Blackbirds. The other day he received from one of his deputy wardens in that same section the head of a male Wood Duck in full plumage, with the request that he have it identified—a task which any twelve-year-old could have performed thirty years ago. (Dawson 1903)

Some people were even fearing the wood ducks' extinction.

It seems only a question of time when the Wood Duck will have followed the Great Auk, Labrador Duck, and others to the land of extinction. (Knight 1908)

The WOOD-DUCK (*Aix sponsa*), by many bird-lovers regarded as the most beautiful of all American birds, is threatened with extinction. . . . (Hornaday 1913)

From the foregoing evidence it can be seen that the Wood Duck, although existing in California in considerable numbers in the early days, is now nearly extinct. (Grinnell 1918)

[T]his lovely species, formerly so abundant, was brought to the point of extinction. (Kortright 1943)

The issue of extinction involves some geographic perspective, however. In many parts of the country, especially in the eastern states, wood ducks were locally rare to locally extinct. It was in the big eastern cities where most conservationists lived that the alarm was sounded the loudest. It was also near large eastern metropolitan areas that market hunting was often most intense and where wildlife populations were most depressed.

Hunters do face a lot of the blame for the situation.

Being shot at all seasons of the year they are becoming very scarce and are likely to be exterminated before long. (Grinnell 1901)

It should be noted that spring and summer shooting was not illegal in the 1800s and early 1900s. These hunters were not criminals. Even today's most ethical hunters, had they lived then, might have harvested what now seems by modern standards a ridiculous number of birds. At the time, however, wildlife and land were thought to be inexhaustible. Hunters fed the masses, just as farmers did.

The plight of the wood duck became a rallying cry for many who opposed hunting or at least opposed some of the excesses of market hunting.

Apparently, the only winged creatures that are too beautiful or too good to be shot and eaten are angels. (Hornaday 1904)

[O]ur people have ruthlessly destroyed this, one of the most beautiful objects of creation, and will yet eradicate it unless laws are enacted and enforced. . . . (Forbush 1912)

Some did see spring hunting as unethical. Spring hunting even inspired a young Aldo Leopold to take up the cause for wildlife in a March 21, 1904, letter to his mother when he was only a teenager. "I am very sorry that ducks are being slaughtered as usual, but of course could expect nothing else. When my turn comes to have something to say and do against it and other related matters I am sure that nothing in my power will be lacking to the good cause" (quoted in A. Leopold 2013).

To put this in context, however, many reports in the late 1800s and early 1900s stated that wood ducks were far from rare in many other regions of the country.

Considerable numbers still nest in favorable localities in the central and northern parts of the state, and in a few places in southern Wisconsin, as about Delavan Lake. (Kumlien and Hollister 1903)

It is extremely common, for instance, about shallow sloughs in heavy hardwood growths along the Mississippi in northeastern Louisiana. (Beyer et al. 1907)

The consensus of opinion is that the Wood Duck has become alarmingly scarce . . . although, in some localities near the center of distribution of the species, the reports were not quite so alarming. (Dutcher 1907)

In the Sunken Lands [Arkansas] it finds ideal nesting haunts, and there it breeds abundantly. (A. H. Howell 1911)

[O]ccasionally the squeak of Wood Ducks could be heard in the stream, which fairly teemed with them. (Kennard 1915)

Fortunately there are still vast areas in the Carolinas, Georgia, Florida, and the Gulf States, where this duck is resident and fairly common . . . and so long as large timbered swamps remain, the species will continue to exist locally in considerable numbers. (Phillips 1925)

I had occasion to take a horseback ride through that region about forty years ago. . . . In that twenty-mile ride the wood ducks were never out of sight, pair on pair, unafraid, looking up idly as they paddled about. (Askins 1931)

By the 1940s, wood ducks had responded well to the protection provided by the Migratory Bird Treaty Act. A limited season was reopened in many states starting in 1942.

We don't know exactly how much wood ducks were impacted by market hunting. If you're a market hunter whose living depends on how many birds you can ship to market, you're going to go to big waters to shoot big flocks of big ducks. Records show wood ducks for sale in the markets of New Orleans (Philips 1925), Boston (Audubon 1840), and Philadelphia (Wilson 1939). However, the more typical targets for market hunters were ducks like mallards and canvasbacks.

While a great many wood ducks are shot, they are nowhere so sufficiently numerous to make it worth while to gun especially for them. Those that are killed are taken chiefly by accident, when they fly near decoys put out for other fowl. (Grinnell 1901)

The records are hazy on how important the wood duck was to market hunting. The species, because of its small size, occurrence in small flocks, and preference for swamps and rivers, certainly was not sought with the ardor shown for the larger and more abundant species found on open waters. (Hester and Dermid 1973)

A means of assessing the extent of market hunters' focus on wood ducks is hinted at in Grinnell's mention of decoys. Decoys for mallard, canvasback, and other heavily hunted species are relatively common in the collectibles market. Wood duck decoys are a different matter. Mackey (1965) writes that "they are so scattered that finding them is sheer luck." Later he writes:

> Doubtless the choicest Mason decoy yet found is the Wood Duck drake. . . . A "Premier" model in mint condition, it must lead the field as a unique and superb specimen. It was discovered by the writer in a gunning shed in the tidewater New Jersey, which is far from a favored habitat of the Wood Duck. Furthermore, it had the company of no handmade Wood Ducks, and the owner of the shack had never bothered to use it. (Mackey 1965)

In a survey of twelve books on waterfowl decoys, wood ducks made up only 0.7 and 1.3 percent, respectively, of the decoys represented in books on the Mississippi and Atlantic Flyways. And even these numbers may be misleading if the books' authors were trying to emphasize the rarer decoys.

The modern hunting story around wood ducks is much different. Today, especially in the Mississippi and Atlantic Flyways, woodies are commonly harvested. The U.S. Fish and Wildlife Service divides the continent into four north-south flyways: Pacific, Central, Mississippi, and Atlantic. The most accurate harvest tracking data begin in 1999, providing about two decades of data on harvest rates for wood ducks. Starting in the Atlantic Flyway, wood ducks have averaged 22.5 percent of the duck harvest since 1999. In the Mississippi Flyway, woodies account for 11.2 percent of ducks harvested. The numbers really drop off in the Central and Pacific Flyways, with wood ducks making up only 2.8 and 1.5 percent of the duck harvest, respectively, since 1999.

Looking at numbers of birds harvested annually, the Mississippi Flyway has been the winner over the last two decades, with an average of 690,100 wood ducks harvested. Hunters in the Atlantic Flyway harvested on average 369,300 wood ducks. Hunters in the Central and Pacific Flyways harvested an annual average of 70,200 and 43,400 wood ducks, respectively, since 1999. Although they are distributed across the continent, wood ducks really are a bird of the eastern half of the continent.

In the Atlantic Flyway, the top three harvest states and their average harvest from 2014 to 2017 are North Carolina (119,300), Georgia (84,600), and South Carolina (76,900). Over these years the wood duck was the most harvested duck in these three states and in the Atlantic Flyway. Wood ducks even outranked the mallard. In 2016 and 2017, wood ducks accounted for 51 and 71 percent of the total duck harvest in North Carolina. To add context, North Carolina hunters are allowed to harvest three wood ducks and four mallards.

In the Mississippi Flyway, the top three states over the last four years and average harvest are Minnesota (119,200), Wisconsin (94,500), and Louisiana (80,100). From 2014 to 2017, wood ducks ranked fifth, third, fourth, and fourth among ducks harvested in the Mississippi Flyway. Here, too, the harvest on woodies is more restrictive than the harvest on some other species.

From fears of extinction, to a ban on all hunting for more than two decades, to numbers like this is an incredible conservation story.

* * * *

One important issue for managing any wildlife population, but especially hunted species, is monitoring their populations. Monitoring helps guide management or conservation strategies as well as sets harvest guidelines.

For many species of ducks that nest across the open Prairie Pothole Region, or Duck Factory, in the north-central part of the United States and the south-central Canadian provinces, biologists fly established transects every year. They record birds detected as well as habitat conditions, such as the number of wetlands. For species such as some Arctic nesting geese, biologists will fly over and count birds in nesting colonies.

Clearly, in no case are biologists counting every bird. They are simply getting population estimates and indices. We don't know exactly how many mallards breed across the Prairie Pothole Region, but we can know that there were more mallards this year than last year, that mallards are some percentage above or below the long-term average, or that there are more mallards in this area compared to that area.

Because their habitat is small, secluded, cluttered, and often covered overhead with trees, it's nearly impossible to get a good count of wood ducks over a reasonable area. It doesn't help that their breeding is scattered across the eastern half of the continent and in the Pacific Northwest instead of being somewhat concentrated in the northern Plains. Brakhage (1988) identified seven types of surveys for wood ducks across fifteen states; nest-box checks, brood counts, nightlighting, breeding pair surveys, stream float counts, habitat surveys, and breeding waterfowl surveys. Sixteen states did not survey wood duck populations. Brakhage concludes his report on these surveys by noting that there isn't a systematic or widely accepted way to survey this species.

Even within each of these methods, the specifics can differ. Survey transects could be different lengths at different times of year in different areas. Methods such as nest-box surveys give us good information on local population dynamics, but it's difficult to say that a nest-box success rate along one stretch of one creek represents the entire region, state, or flyway. Zimmerman et al. (2015) proposed estimating wood duck populations by combining the Atlantic Flyway Breeding Waterfowl Survey (AFBWS) and the Breeding Bird Survey (BBS) approaches. AFBWS are based on surveys of plots, and BBS are based on routes or transects. BBS routes are poor at estimating wood duck populations because few wood ducks are recorded on these surveys due to its living in habitats that make detection difficult. Their results aligned relatively well with population estimates derived from harvests. Studies taken together can be more revealing than isolated study results. No one survey is perfect, but when researchers combine different surveys, each using different methods, the larger analysis will be stronger than the results of individual methods.

Population estimates from harvesting are based largely on banding returns. One trophy prized by many waterfowl hunters are the leg bands they find on some birds. A trophy for a waterfowl hunter is a data point for a waterfowl biologist. Banding is really hard work. It takes many hours and a lot of people to do it safely. People must scout locations to see where birds have been in recent days. Traps are set, baited, and monitored. Then there is the actual banding. Birds can be captured for banding in many ways, including nightlighting and netting, swim-in or walk-in traps, and rocket-netting. Bands range in size from those appropriate for the smallest sparrows and warblers all the way up to those that fit trumpeter swans. Wood ducks require a band size 5A. For context, blue-winged teal require a 4A band; mallards and canvasbacks require a 7A band; Canada geese require 7B-8 bands; and trumpeter swans require a 9-9c band (Pyle 2008).

Having someone find a band and report it is a low probability result, so biologists must band a lot of birds to get a few returns. With large datasets, biologists can create robust and accurate statistical models, but as the numbers get smaller, the models become less accurate and less useful. Biologists also want to put bands on the right birds. "Right" in this case means numbers of the year's males and females, adult and young, that will allow scientists to get the most out of their models. Kelley (2003) reports that from 1992 to 1995, biologists in Illinois, Iowa, Minnesota, Missouri, and Wisconsin were able to band sufficient numbers of adult and juvenile males, but only banded 45 and 85 percent, respectively, of the adult and juvenile females necessary to make their models as robust as they would have liked.

Banding birds has a long tradition in world history (Lincoln 1921; Cole 1922; Wood 1945). In western Europe, bird banding dates back to at least the sixteenth century. Banding in Asia and the Middle East may go back even earlier. Many of the earliest birds to be banded were falcons, for the very practical reason of establishing a falconer's ownership or potentially aiding in the recovery of an escaped bird. One of the earliest records of banding in the Americas was provided by a young Audubon, who placed a silver thread on nestling phoebes in 1803 and recovered adult birds the next year that had his thread on their legs.

The early history of bird banding in the United States includes several players, but the most important is probably Frederick Lincoln, who was with the U.S. Biological Survey, now the U.S. Fish and Wildlife Service. Lincoln developed the nationwide system of distributing, recording, and re-porting band recoveries. He would eventually go on to develop the flyway concept as well as the Lincoln Index, which allows scientists to estimate the population of any wildlife species using the number of marked individuals and the number of recovered individuals. His index is still used today.

From banding data, biologists can estimate harvest distribution, where birds are recovered, and harvest derivation, that is, where the harvested birds came from. Biologists can also calculate recovery and harvest rates. Putting this all together, they can start to estimate regional, flyway, and continental populations. Harvest, seasons, and bag limits can be adjusted to ensure birds aren't overharvested. Of course, models aren't perfect, and what should count as overharvest has been debated.

Several studies have looked at banding recoveries. There are two types of recoveries. Direct recoveries indicate birds were harvested or recaptured the same year they were banded. Indirect recoveries indicate birds were harvested or recaptured more than a year later. Many banding efforts focus on captur-ing young of the year birds, allowing researchers to determine where birds hatched in one area move to. Researchers use banding to develop life tables and age distributions of wildlife species. Their data can also help determine the maximum age of individuals. Looking at birds banded as hatch-year birds, the Bird Banding Laboratory lists a twenty-two-year-old wood duck banded in Oregon and recovered in California and two thirteen-year-old birds. One of these birds was hatched in Iowa and recovered in Louisiana, while the other one was hatched in Illinois and recovered in Wisconsin. Two birds banded as adults were at least seventeen and thirteen years old. Obviously, birds this old are the rare exceptions, not the rule.

Wood ducks have been banded and banded ducks recovered in all of the continental states. They aren't evenly distributed across those states, how-ever. Between 1960 and 2018, researchers and managers banded 1,711,100 wood ducks. During that same period, 217,400 banded wood ducks—only 12.7 percent of bands—were recovered. And that's actually a relatively large number compared to songbird studies, since people don't harvest songbirds each fall, researchers must rely on recaptured birds or dead birds that have been found and reported.

Since 1960, Iowa has banded more than 153,000 wood ducks, the most of any state. Illinois and Tennessee come in second and third with 138,800 and 103,800 wood ducks banded. Minnesota, Kentucky, Wisconsin, Ohio, and Louisiana have banded between 80,000 and 90,000 woodies. When it comes to recovering banded wood ducks, Louisiana leads with 27,200. South Carolina and Iowa round out the top three with 14,000 and 12,600. North Carolina (12,200), Wisconsin (11,800), Georgia (11,500), Arkansas (11,100), and Minnesota (10,600) are the other states with over ten thousand bands recovered. Grice and Rogers (1965) report that wood ducks banded in Massachusetts were found in all the states that border the Atlantic Ocean as well as in Louisiana, Mississippi, Alabama, Tennessee, Michigan, Ontario, and Nova Scotia. Beshears (1974) found that ducks banded in Alabama (Mississippi Flyway) were recovered in all Mississippi Flyway states except Missouri, in all but three Atlantic Flyway states, in two Central

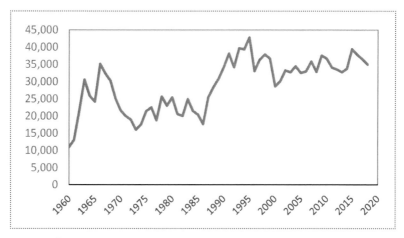

Number of wood ducks banded annually across all states since 1960. Year to year variation may represent either changes in duck populations or in banding efforts. Data downloaded from Bird Band Laboratory website.

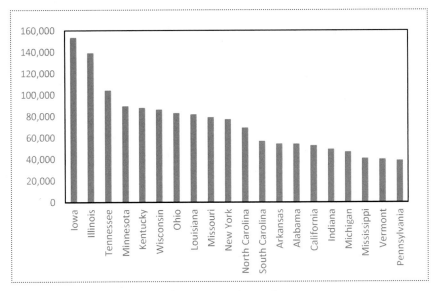

Number of wood ducks banded in the top states since 1960.

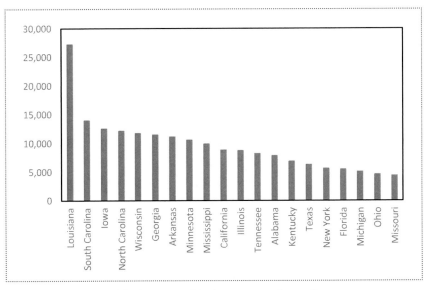

Number of banded wood ducks recovered in the top states since 1960.

Flyway states, and in two Canadian provinces. Birds banded in five Canadian provinces and twenty-eight states have been recovered in Alabama. Wood ducks banded in Louisiana between 1949 and 1976 were recovered in twenty-five states and provinces. Banded wood ducks recovered in Louisiana were from every state of the Mississippi Flyway, all but two states in the Atlantic Flyway, three Canadian provinces, and the six states stretching from North Dakota to Texas in the Central Flyway (Bateman 1977). Hayden and Pollock (1988) found similar results for birds banded and recovered in Alabama. Havera (1999) provides detailed maps of recoveries for several species banded in Illinois. Indirect recoveries of Illinois banded wood ducks were recorded from fourteen states in the Mississippi Flyway, eleven states in the Atlantic Flyway, five states in the Central Flyway, and one state in the Pacific Flyway, as well as from three Canadian provinces. Direct recoveries were recorded in thirteen, four, and five states of the Mississippi, Atlantic, and Central Flyways, respectively.

Fuller (1975) studied direct recoveries of birds banded in North Carolina. Conventional wisdom states that birds banded in the summer should be harvested in the fall somewhere farther south. Everyone knows that birds go south for the winter. Indeed, the strong majority of North Carolina banded birds were recovered in North Carolina, South Carolina, and Georgia. However, birds were recovered in twenty-five states and one Canadian province. Ten of these states were in the Atlantic Flyway and one was in the Central Flyway. Some birds actually go north in the late summer and early fall. And then there are some really oddball ducks that must have gotten lost. Rondeau (2007) tells of a duck banded on June 30, 2005, near Butte, California, as a young of the year bird. It was recaptured seventy-one days later on September 9 in Fergus Falls, Minnesota. Bateman (1977) has records of hatch-year birds banded in Louisiana and recovered the same fall in Wisconsin and South Carolina.

What does this say about the flyway concept if birds born in one flyway can be recovered in other flyways? The flyways are just statistical estimates; there will always be outliers. For instance, Fuller's North Carolina study found that more than eight hundred, two hundred, and five hundred banded birds, respectively, were recovered in North Carolina, South Carolina, and Georgia. Louisiana, Mississippi, and Alabama had forty-four, sixteen, and sixty-one recoveries, respectively, and the rest of the Mississippi Flyway states had recoveries in the single digits. In the data from Illinois reported by Havera, 89 percent of the direct recoveries and 85 percent of the indirect recoveries were in the Mississippi Flyway. So, yes, the flyway concept generally holds up.

* * * *

Once a bird is harvested, the dog has retrieved it to hand, and you've admired the feathers up close, more can be learned from each bird. The first thing a hunter can do is to age the bird, determining if it is young of the year or an adult bird.

Hunters can look at the wings of any duck to determine its age. Sam Carney's *Species, Age, and Sex Identification of Ducks Using Wing Plumage* (1992) is available online and can be downloaded. This reference provides a key for every species of duck. Briefly, in juvenile wood ducks, the tertial feathers will be more pointed than those in the adults. In adult birds, the blue iridescence extends to the third row of covert and extends farther toward the tip of the wing. Other subtler differences are best studied by comparing a specimen to photos of wings of known age. The tail feathers can also reveal the bird's age. If some of the tail feathers, rectrices, have small notches at the tips, the duck is a juvenile. The notches are formed when the natal plume break off (Pyle 2008).

In addition to aging the wings, hunters should carefully examine the top sections of the digestive tract to determine what the birds in the area have been eating recently: acorns, corn, or duckweed. The information could help guide the hunter in deciding where to hunt the next day.

9 engagement

My husband and I find the best way to spend our holidays is to take some tools, instruments and climbers, then off to the woods we go to study wild nature.—*Bendick 1931*

It took two and a half hours to get the young to water, a distance of two blocks. . . . Finally a traffic officer held up cars passing on the road and curious people were kept back. . . . It was only a few minutes before they were all following her safely across the road to the river.—*Gigstead 1938*

Everybody in that little river town knew of this nest, and the moment the first duckling crawled out of the nest hole, squeaking in its excitement, all traffic along the state highway was stopped or detoured for the several hours necessary for all the baby birds to scramble out of the nest cavity and for the mother to lead them safely across the dangerous concrete road, then down the bank into the slowly flowing Illinois River.—*Musselman 1948*

My nesting project has had substantial local newspaper publicity through a neighbor who, for years, was editor of our daily paper. As a result, many citizens have become interested and have erected nesting boxes.—*F. Leopold 1966*

This penultimate chapter should start with words from the concluding chapter of Aldo Leopold's *Game Management* (1933): "The game manager manipulates animals and vegetation to produce a game crop. This however, is only a superficial indication of his social significance. What he really labors for is to bring about a new attitude toward the land." This sentiment would of course undergo further development to become the Land Ethic. These quotes, and many others, demonstrate Leopold's "indirect hidden-hand" in wood duck conservation that Art Hawkins wrote about. If nothing else, an interest in wood ducks, nest boxes, and other aspects of the wood duck's life history should help anyone develop or further refine their attitude toward the land and their own Land Ethic.

Conservation is hard work. It's darn hard work. It's really expensive, often takes a long time, and often happens someplace far away. Most of us don't have millions of dollars to spend to buy and protect land. We don't have the licenses needed to operate a bulldozer to restore wetlands. We don't have the training, certifications, or specialized equipment and vehicles to conduct prescribed burns to enhance nesting habitat. The politics and science of conservation usually requires specific education, training, and experience.

Yes, writing a check to a national or local conservation organization is a good thing to do. But it doesn't leave a person with a lot of visceral satisfaction. People want to DO something. They literally want to get their hands dirty. In the evening, a blister on a thumb or a sore back is simply the evidence that good things were accomplished that day.

Too often wildlife management is left up to agency staff. Especially in today's world of ringing phones, emails, meetings, reports, plans, and budgets, just about every wildlife agency staff wishes they could spend more time in the field. Ask any agency wildlife biologist or manager if they would rather be in the field or answering emails. Guess which they would choose.

Consider the two comments below on nest boxes. The first notes that large nest-box programs can be taxing on agency staff and resources. The second describes nest boxes as the most natural way for the general public to participate in conservation activities. Put another way, if an agency biologist tried to build and maintain one hundred boxes, he wouldn't get much else done for several weeks each year. But if ten private citizens each built and maintained ten boxes, they would each have a nice hobby and a way to engage in conservation.

> However, large numbers of the houses must be placed out to materially attract and increase wood duck populations, and considerable time and expense would be involved in constructing, checking, and cleaning the structures. Their use is recommended to the *extent of available time and means*. . . . (Dill 1966)

Protection had much to do with this comeback, but that alone is never quite enough. It must be leavened with some positive, hands-on management, and the wood duck was a natural for this—presenting one of those rare and classic situations in wildlife management where everything comes into focus. This was something the outdoor public could readily understand, sympathize with, and really do something about. . . . Ah, for the sweet, lost days when private citizens could become so personally involved in practical game management, with such gratifying results. (Madson 1985)

As we've seen throughout this book, sometimes wood ducks make their homes near people. And sometimes, people make their homes near wood ducks. Ask a modern-day realtor about the abundance of wood ducks at a potential new house and you might get some strange looks.

A sister, who was with me at the time I definitely decided to make my permanent home on the lake where I live to-day, declares that I paid the purchase price for an acre of blue-eyed grass, which I acquired with my holdings. She is only partly right. A wood duck also figured into the equation. (Porter 1919)

In other cases, the presence of wood ducks was a happy surprise for the new homeowner.

Shortly after moving into a new home along the Mississippi River just north of Minneapolis, I became aware of several pairs of wood ducks nesting in hollow basswood trees on the nearby river banks. (Breckenridge 1956)

Wood duck conservation can engage the individual who builds a nest box or an entire community as described in the quotes at the beginning of this chapter. Wood duck conservation doesn't happen in some far-off place that we'll never see or only occasionally visit. It often happens right here, wherever your here is. Wood duck conservation can occur literally in your back yard, or at least someplace a short distance away from many of us.

Several of the most popular locations are less than 20 feet from two homes. In fact, I placed one box so I could see it clearly through a window in my bedroom when my head rested on the pillow. (F. Leopold 1966)

It was not until our third spring (1942), however, that we discovered a pair of these beautiful ducks nested in a certain basswood about 100 feet from our breakfast nook. (Breckenridge 1946)

We have had over 100 wood ducks eating acorns on our lawn at one time. (Bradley 1985)

But even when they are that close, they still insist that we be carefully observant.

One natural cavity that we did discover is less than thirty feet directly opposite our kitchen window. In a single season, a hen makes twenty or more trips to and from the nest to lay her eggs and well over a hundred additional trips during the incubation of the eggs. In all these many trips each year to and from the nest near the cabin, so stealthy were the hen's movements that we never once noticed her. (Shurtleff and Savage 1996)

Building a nesting box is one of the easiest ways people can actively engage and participate in conservation. Building a box involves a trip to the lumber store, tools, and time in the workshop. Those are activities many of us enjoy. Building boxes can involve some quiet thoughtful time alone in the shop (with a dog underfoot of course), quality time with a kid or grandkid, or a community service project involving many people.

Building nest boxes, talking to local conservation experts about general places to hang boxes, walking or canoeing along a creek or the edge of a lake near home to find specific locations to hang boxes, and then hanging the boxes are some of the best ways to engage people in conservation.

My nesting project has had substantial local newspaper publicity through a near neighbor who, for years, was the editor of our daily paper. (F. Leopold 1966)

(*Right*)
The next generation of conservation-
ists build nest boxes as part of the
Minnesota Waterfowl Association's
(MWA) week-long "Woodie Camp."
Photo courtesy MWA.

(*Below*)
The Fergus Falls (Minnesota) Fish
and Game Club and their efforts to
increase wood ducks in the local area.
Building and selling boxes serves as a
fundraising project for the club.
Photo courtesy of Tony Rondeau.

Checking, monitoring, keeping records, cleaning, and repairing boxes are some of the best ways to keep people engaged.

[N]est boxes represent an important and tangible means by which conservation-minded individuals or groups can make significant contributions to the welfare of these beautiful birds. (Bellrose 1953)

Our research has generated interest in wood ducks and other cavity nesters among people of all ages. Youngsters have developed construction and photographic skills and techniques for scientific research and observation. Adults have increased their appreciation of this remarkable bird. Everyone gains a feeling of pride from participating in these projects. The same rewards await anyone who enters in the life of a woodie. (Bradley 1985)

A wood duck nest-house program can be personally rewarding, educational, and locally effective. . . . Erecting nest houses is also a means to involve the public in simple wildlife management and, in some instances, increase communication between agencies and the public. (Soulliere 1986)

But wildlife managers and interested citizens working together can help shape the course of events. Citizen participation in wood duck nest box programs is a good start in the right direction. (Hawkins et al. 1988)

Once you're hooked on wood ducks and want to put up some boxes, it's easy to let your heart get in front of your head, doing too much too fast. Start small with a few boxes. If successful, gradually add a few boxes every few years. But don't overwhelm yourself. To maintain the hobbyist's interest, a hobby should be fun and informative. Once it becomes a chore, your nest-box program will have less success. Bateman (1977) italicized a warning in his manual for Louisiana wood duck enthusiasts, cautioning them not to erect more boxes than they can maintain.

Erecting and maintaining a small number of nest boxes will usually result in better long-term use, success, and personal satisfaction than a greater number of unattended boxes. Whatever you do, keep it interesting and enjoyable for you, your family and friends. (Nelson 2001)

It is amazing what some individuals have been able to do. From 1943 to 1977, Frederic Leopold hatched 4,624 ducklings in Burlington, Iowa. From 1980 to 2000, 3,378 ducklings left Harvey Nelson's boxes in Bloomington, Minnesota.

This is where citizen engagement can play such an important role. Individuals, Scout troops, civic groups, and conservation clubs can all build and maintain nest boxes. They can work together. Someone can buy the materials, another group can build boxes, and others can hang them. Or everyone can participate in every step. It can't stop there, however. If nest boxes are a gateway, the gateway must lead to other involvement.

Anyone who inspects boxes after the nesting season and records data on how many eggs of what species hatched in them is a citizen scientist. These numbers become ever more interesting as the years pass and you can tally up the number of ducklings produced through your efforts. Support conservation groups. Write those checks. Talk to local, state, and federal politicians. Talk to neighbors and friends. Volunteer at your nearby wildlife agency office.

Wood ducks allow us into their lives as few other wildlife and almost no other duck allows. We can watch the comings and goings of the hen in the spring. If we're lucky, we can watch the ducklings launch out of the hole. Later in the summer, we can watch the hen and her brood leave trails through the duckweed.

Building a box with a kid or grandkid, hanging the box, recording data from the box, and then watching their reactions as they watch a brood of THEIR ducklings from THEIR nest box. . . . One or two experiences like that and kids will be hooked and engaged for life on ducks, wildlife, and conservation.

* * * *

One important aspect of engagement is keeping records. This could be done using pen and paper, by typing into a computer, or by sharing information electronically with many friends. As a rebel against being chained to a computer most days, when at home I do as much with pen and paper as I can.

Detailed records of your conservation story will be very rewarding in the future, when you will be able to look back at your experiences yourself or share them with kids, grandkids, and others. Here are two versions of a possible story recording some of Frederic Leopold's efforts on behalf of wood ducks.

VERSION 1.

Frederic hung three nest boxes in the yard and hatched broods of ducks from each box.

VERSION 2.

When Frank Bellrose and Art Hawkins, the latter a former student of Frederic's brother Aldo Leopold, started their wood duck research in the spring of 1938, they gave Frederic fifty nest boxes. He hung them at Crystal Lake Hunt Club, where his father, brothers, and he had hunted ducks for decades. He placed boxes at Black Jack Point, East Run Point, Schlapp's Island, Pin Oaks, Youngs Island, west of Stoney Lake, Phillips Well, north of Phillips Well, northwest of Youngs Well, Flat Foot, Wundt's Island, and Picnic Point.

In the early spring of 1943, Art Hawkins was visiting the Leopold house in Burlington, Iowa. Frederic and Art were enjoying breakfast when they saw through the bay window a pair of wood ducks land in the larch tree in the yard. Art and Frederic both thought the same thing: The ducks were looking for a nesting site.

Frederic shortly after crossed the Mississippi River to Crystal Lake and removed three nest boxes. He hung them in the larch tree south of the porch, in the red oak on the bluff edge on the southeast corner of the property, and in the pine on the terrace northeast of the house.

He saw the first wood ducks on April 10. On April 29, he inspected each nest box. The first box contained eight eggs, the second held twelve eggs, and there were six eggs in the third house. Eggs hatched on June third, first, and fourth, respectively.

The second is obviously a much richer story, and I was only able to create it because Frederic kept such careful and detailed notes over the years (F. Leopold 1953, 1984). His notes contain more than just tables and numbers and statistics. They do include all of those, but Frederic also wove a narrative throughout that, together with his numbers, tells a revealing and memorable story.

conclusion still water

Wood duck habitat isn't easy, but it invites an intimacy. Some people seem to take comfort from spending time in it. Audubon (1840) took "peculiar pleasure" in watching wood ducks in their habitat. Wood duck habitat is small, secluded. It's characterized by mud, downed trees, branches hidden just under the water's surface ready to trip you or rip a hole in your waders. It's not a fun place for a casual stroll. James Kilgo (1988) describes walking in a wood duck marsh as "going fast and slow at the same time."

Especially if you live in the eastern half of the country, wood duck habitat may not be too far from home. It's often quite close, although off the road, across the field, behind some trees, and hidden from view. In "Smoky Gold" (1949), Aldo Leopold describes a stolen grouse hunt taking place in "some undiscovered place under everyone's nose." That's often one of the best places to find wood ducks. You may find them just a little off the beaten path.

Waterfowl stories are often told as big adventures: big boats with big outboards on big waters, big flights over big fields under bigger skies, and sometimes big risks and narrow escapes. High drama. Often when looking for ducks, we can simply scan wetlands from a distance with binoculars or a spotting scope. Rafts of ducks in open water are easy to find. Wood ducks hidden in their haunts are rarely seen from a distance. Finding them requires exploration. It often requires trading the guttural roar of an outboard for the dip of a paddle or boots and paws crunching leaves, sucking mud, or splashing rivulets. Finding wood ducks isn't easy, but nothing worth having ever is.

The fly-fishing literature has its one pure, perfect sentence: Norman Maclean's *"I am haunted by waters."* No waterfowl writer has yet achieved that mastery. While other writers use the word "quiet," two other words even more evocative of the mood and feel of wood ducks keep repeating throughout the wood duck literature.

> . . . its favorite haunts being the solitary, deep, and still water, ponds, woody lakes, and mill-dams. . . . (Chamberlain 1891)

> Deep flooded swamps where ancient mossy trees overhang the dark still waters, secluded pools amid the scattered pines where water-lilies lift their snowy heads and turtles bask in the sun. (Forbush 1925)

The following quotes from Chuck Petrie's essay "Reflections on a Wood Duck Pond" and Wendell Berry's poem "The Peace of Wild Things" probably best describe the therapeutic effects of finding where the wood ducks are and going there yourself.

> Reflections on a wood duck pond seem to take the harshness out of reality—not necessarily distorting it but softening it, at least temporarily. Sitting on the bank of a stream, watching the current go by, I often get a hopeless feeling of being left behind by time. Here, though, where there is no current, just still water, and solitude, my mind follows time in any direction, and I can believe that all is right with my life, that the future will be gentle, and my past, when necessary, has been forgiven. (Petrie 1987)

I go and lie down where the wood drake
rests in his beauty on the water, and the great heron feeds.
I come into the peace of wild things
who do not tax their lives with forethought
of grief. I come into the presence of still water. (Berry 1968)

It is interesting how often the words "still water" are used in the context of wood ducks. Of course, each of these writers was probably consciously or unconsciously thinking of David's writing in the Twenty-third Psalm, which in my Grandma's King James reads, "He leadeth me beside the still waters."

If nothing else, I hope this book inspires you to actively engage in conservation in your own way and to find your spot on the map of your personal geography, with its own still water. Who knows what you'll see, find, or learn there. Go find the place where your wood drake rests in his beauty.

bibliography

Abrams, M. D. 1992. "Fire and the Development of Oak Forests." *Bioscience* 42 (5): 346–353.

Abrams, M. D. 2003. "Where Has All the White Oak Gone?" *Bioscience* 53 (10): 927–939.

Allen, C. E. 1980. "Feeding Habits of Ducks in a Green-Tree Reservoir in Eastern Texas." *Journal of Wildlife Management* 44 (1): 232–236.

Anderson, J. T., and T. C. Tacha. 2002. "Habitat Use by Nonbreeding Wood Ducks in the Coastal Plain and Rice Prairie Region of Texas." *Southwestern Naturalist* 47 (3): 486–489.

Anonymous. 1886. "The Destruction of Birds for Millinery Purposes." *Science* 7 (160): 196–197.

Armbruster, J. S. 1982. "Wood Duck Displays and Pairing Chronology." *Auk* 99 (1): 116–122.

Askins, C. 1931. *Game Bird Shooting*. New York: Macmillan.

Audubon, J. J. 1840. *The Birds of America*. New York: John James Audubon.

Bahls, J., and J. Bartholmai. 2013. "Buffleheads Nesting on Wisconsin's Horicon Marsh—2013." *Wood Duck Newsgram*, November, 9.

Bailey, F. M. 1902. *Handbook of the Birds of the Western United States*. New York: Houghton, Mifflin.

Baird, S. F., T. M. Brewer, and R. Ridgway. 1884. *The Water Birds of North America. Memoirs of the Museum of Comparative Zoology, Vol XIII*. Boston: Little, Brown.

Baldassarre, G. 2014. *Ducks, Geese, and Swans of North America*. Baltimore: Johns Hopkins University Press.

Ball, I. J., D. S. Gilmer, L. M. Cowardin, and J. H. Riechmann. 1975. "Survival of Wood Duck and Mallard Broods in North-Central Minnesota." *Journal of Wildlife Management* 39 (4): 776–780.

Barras, S. C., R. M. Kaminski, and L. A. Brennan. 1996. "Acorn Selection by Female Wood Ducks." *Journal of Wildlife Management* 60 (3): 592–602.

Bateman, H. A. 1977. *The Wood Duck in Louisiana*. Baton Rouge: Louisiana Department of Wildlife and Fisheries.

Beard, E. B. 1964. "Duck Brood Behavior at the Seney National Wildlife Refuge." *Journal of Wildlife Management* 28 (3): 492-521.

Behrens, R. R. 2018. *Under the Big Top at Sims' Circus: Ship Camouflage behind the Scenes in World War One.* Cedar Falls: Hearst Center for the Arts. Published in conjunction with an exhibition of camouflage artifacts, *The Work of Dazzle Camouflage,* Hearst Center for the Arts, October 5, 2018-November 25, 2018.

Bellrose, F. 1953. "Housing for Wood Ducks." *Illinois Natural History Survey.* Circular 45. Champaign: Illinois Natural History Survey.

Bellrose, F. 1976. *The Ducks, Geese, and Swans of North America.* Harrisburg, PA: Stackpole Books.

Bellrose, F., and D. Holm. 1994. *Ecology and Management of the Wood Duck.* Mechanicsburg, PA: Stackpole Books.

Bellrose, F. C. 1966. Remarks of the Chairman. In *Wood Duck Management and Research: A Symposium,* 4-5. Washington, D.C.: Wildlife Management Institute.

Bellrose, F. C., K. L. Johnston, and T. U. Meyers. 1964. "Relative Value of Natural Cavities and Nesting Houses for Wood Ducks." *Journal of Wildlife Management* 28 (4): 661-676.

Bellrose, F., S. Nielsen, and R. McCabe. 1993. *The Unique Wood Duck.* Mechanicsburg, PA: Stackpole Books.

Bendick, A. M. 1931. "The Wood Duck." *The Game Breeder,* December, 377-379.

Benson, D., and F. C. Bellrose. 1964. "Eastern Production Areas." In *Waterfowl Tomorrow,* edited by J. P. Linduska, 89-98. Washington, D.C.: U.S. Fish and Wildlife Service.

Bent, A. C. 1951. *Life Histories of North American Wild Fowl, Vol. 1.* New York: Dover.

Berry, W. 1968. *Openings.* New York: Harcourt, Brace.

Beshears, W. W. 1974. *Wood Ducks in Alabama.* Special Report No. 4. A contribution of Federal Aid in Wildlife Restoration, Final Report, Project W-35, Job I-F. Montgomery: Alabama Division of Game and Fish.

Beyer, G. E., A. Allison, and H. Kopman. 1907. "List of the Birds of Louisiana. Part III." *Auk* 24 (3): 314-321.

Blanchan, N. 1905. *Birds That Hunt and Are Hunted: Life Histories of One Hundred and Seventy Birds of Prey, Game Birds, and Water-fowls.* New York: Doubleday.

Bogardus, A. 1878. *Field, Cover, and Trap Shooting.* Reprinted, Prescott, AZ: Wolfe.

Bonar, R. L. 2000. "Availability of Pileated Woodpecker Cavities and Use by Other Species." *Journal of Wildlife Management* 64 (1): 52-59.

Bowers, E. F., and J. S. Atkins. 1988. "Nest Height Preference of the Wood Duck." In *The 1988 North American Wood Duck Symposium,* edited by Leigh H. Fredrickson et al., 245-248. Selected papers from the symposium held in St. Louis, Missouri, February 20-22.

Boyer, R. L. 1975. "Wildlife Occupying Potential Wood Duck Tree Nest Sites." *Wilson Bulletin* 87 (4): 558-559.

Bradley, L. 1985. "Your Back Yard: Possible Home for Wood Ducks?" *Minnesota Conservation Volunteer,* March-April, 37-42.

Bradley, L. 1994. "Questions and Answers." *Wood Duck Newsgram,* July, 3-4.

Bradley, L. 2005. "Brush and Branches: Waste or Duck Enhancement." *Wood Duck Newsgram,* November, 4-5.

Brakhage, C. K. 1966. "Management of Mast Crops for Wood Ducks." In *Wood Duck Management and Research: A Symposium,* 75-80. Washington, D.C.: Wildlife Management Institute.

Brakhage, D. H. 1988. "Techniques Currently Used for Monitoring Wood Duck Populations." In *Wood Duck Management and Research: A Symposium,* 201-204. Washington, D.C.: Wildlife Management Institute.

Breckenridge, W. J. 1946. "Wood Duck at the Brackens." *The Flicker* 18 (1): 1-2.

Breckenridge, W. J. 1956. "Nesting Study of Wood Ducks." *Journal of Wildlife Management* 20 (1): 16-21.

Breckenridge, W. J. 1999. "Part 2 of the Annual Cycle of the Wood Duck." *Wood Duck Newsgram,* March, 14-15.

Breckenridge, W. J. 2009. *My Life in Natural History: An Autobiography.* Edited by B. B. Franklin and J. Moriarty. Minneapolis: Special Publication of the J. F. Bell Museum of Natural History, University of Minnesota.

Broschart, M. R., C. A. Johnston, and R. J. Naiman. 1989. "Predicting Beaver Colony Density in Boreal Landscapes." *Journal of Wildlife Management* 53 (4): 929-934.

Brown, L. G., and F. C. Bellrose. 1943. "Use of Nesting Boxes for Wood Duck by Other Wildlife." *Journal of Wildlife Management* 7 (3): 298-306.

Bruette, W. 1930. *American Duck, Goose, and Brant Shooting.* New York: Charles Scribners and Sons.

Burchsted, D., M. Daniels, R. Thorson, and J. Vokoun. 2010. "The River Discontinuum: Applying Beaver Modifications to Baseline Conditions for Restoration of Forested Headwater." *Bioscience* 60 (11): 908-922.

Burroughs, J. 1905. *The Writings of John Burroughs XIV: The Ways of Nature.* Boston: Houghton, Mifflin.

Carney, S. M. 1992. *Species, Age, and Sex Identification of Ducks Using Wing Plumage.* Washington, D.C.: U.S. Fish and Wildlife Service.

Chamberlain, M. 1891. *A Popular Handbook of the Ornithology of the United States and Canada, Vol II: Game and Water Birds.* Boston: Little, Brown.

Chapman, F. 1886. "Birds and Bonnets." *Forest and Stream* 26 (February 25): 84.

Chapman, F. 1907. *Handbook of Birds of Eastern North America.* New York: D. Appleton.

Clawson, R. L., G. W. Hartman, and L. H. Fredrickson. 1979. "Nest Dumping in a Missouri Wood Duck Population." *Journal of Wildlife Management* 43 (2): 347–355.

Clugston, D. A. 1999. "Availability of Nest Cavity Trees for Wood Ducks (*Aix sponsa*) at Sunkhaze Meadows National Wildlife Refuge, Maine." *Northeastern Naturalist* 6 (2): 133–138.

Cole, L. J. 1922. "The Early History of Bird Banding in America." *Wilson Bulletin* 34: 108–114.

Collias, N. E. 1964. "The Evolution of Nests and Nest-building in Birds." *American Zoologist* 4 (2): 175–190.

Conner, R. N., C. E. Shackelford, D. Saenz, and R. R. Schaefer. 2001. "Interactions between Nesting Pileated Woodpeckers and Wood Ducks." *Wilson Bulletin* 113 (2): 250–253.

Cooke, W. W. 1906. *Distribution and Migration of North American Ducks, Geese, and Swans.* Biological Survey-Bulletin No. 26. Washington, D.C.: U.S. Department of Agriculture.

Corrigan, R. M., G. J. Scrimgeour, and C. Paszkowski. 2011. "Nest Boxes Facilitate Local-scale Conservation of Common Goldeneye (*Bucephala clangula*) and Bufflehead (*Bucephala and albeola*) in Alberta, Canada." *Avian Conservation and Biology* 6 (1): http://dx.doi.org/10.5751/ACE-00435-060101.

Cottrell, S. D., H. H. Prince, and P. I. Padding. 1988. "Nest Success, Duckling Survival, and Brood Habitat Selection of Wood Ducks in a Tennessee Riverine System." In *The 1988 North American Wood Duck Symposium,* edited by Leigh H. Fredrickson et al., 191–198. Selected papers from the symposium held in St. Louis, Missouri, February 20–22.

Coulter, M. W. 1955. "Spring Food Habits of Surface-feeding Ducks in Maine." *Journal of Wildlife Management* 19 (2): 263–267.

Coulter, M. W. 1957. "Food of Wood Ducks in Maine." *Journal of Wildlife Management* 21 (2): 235–236.

Cronan, J. M. 1957. "Effects of Predator Guards on Wood Duck Box Usage." *Journal of Wildlife Management* 21(4): 468.

Darwin, C. 1859. *The Origin of Species by Means of Natural Selection.* London: John Murray.

Darwin, C. 1871. *The Descent of Man and Selection in Relation to Sex.* London: John Murray.

Davis, J. B., R. R. Cox, R. M. Kaminski, and B. D. Leopold. 2007. "Survival of Wood Duck Ducklings and Broods in Mississippi and Alabama." *Journal of Wildlife Management* 71 (2): 507–517.

Davis, J. B., B. D. Leopold, R. M. Kaminski, and R. R. Cox. 2009. "Wood Duck Duckling Mortality and Habitat Implications in Floodplain Systems." *Wetlands* 29 (2): 607–614.

Davis, J. B., J. N. Straub, G. Wang, R. M. Kaminski, and B. D. Leopold. 2015. "Simulations of Wood Duck Recruitment from Nest Boxes in Mississippi and Alabama." *Journal of Wildlife Management* 79 (6): 907–916.

Dawson, W. L. 1903. *The Birds of Ohio: A Complete Scientific and Popular Description of the 320 Species of Birds Found in the State.* Columbus: Wheaton Publishing.

Decker, E. 1959. "A 4-year Study of Wood Ducks on a Pennsylvania Marsh." *Journal of Wildlife Management* 23 (3): 310–315.

Delacour, J., and E. Mayr. 1945. "The Family Anatidae." *Wilson Bulletin* 57 (1): 2–55.

Delnicki, D., and K. J. Reinecke. 1986. "Mid-winter Food Use and Body Weights of Mallards and Wood Ducks in Mississippi." *Journal of Wildlife Management* 50 (1): 43–51.

Denton, J. C., C. L. Roy, G. J. Soullierre, and B. A. Potter. 2012. "Current and Projected Abundance of Potential Nest Sites for Cavity-nesting Ducks in Hardwoods of the North Central United States." *Journal of Wildlife Management* 76 (2): 422–432.

Dill, H. H. 1966. "Meeting Management Objectives for Wood Ducks." In *Wood Duck Management and Research: A Symposium,* 81–90. Washington, D.C.: Wildlife Management Institute.

Dingle, H. 1996. *Migration: The Biology of Life on the Move.* New York: Oxford University Press.

Dries, R. E. 1954. "A Field Observation Method of Aging Broods of Wood Ducks." *Journal of Wildlife Management* 18 (2): 280–281.

Drobney, R. D. 1980. "Reproductive Bioenergetics of Wood Ducks." *Auk* 97 (3): 480–490.

Drobney, R. D. 1982. "Body Weight and Composition Changes and Adaptations for Breeding in Wood Ducks." *Condor* 84 (3): 300–305.

Drobney, R. D., and L. H. Fredrickson. 1979. "Food Selection by Wood Ducks in Relation to Breeding Status." *Journal of Wildlife Management* 43 (1): 109–120.

Dutcher, W. 1907. "The Wood Duck." *Bird-Lore* 9 (4): 189–192.

Eaton, E. H. 1910. *Birds of New York.* Albany: University of the State of New York.

Ellis-Felege, S. N., C. G. Skaggs, and G. A. Knutsen. 2018. "Increased Bufflehead (*Bucephala albeola*) Breeding Activity in Minnesota." *Canadian Field-Naturalist* 131 (4): 338–343.

Errington, P. 1937. "A Wood-Duck Marsh in Northwestern Iowa." *Auk* 54 (4): 533–534.

Errington, P. 1987. *A Question of Values.* Ames: Iowa State University Press.

Evans, M. R., D. B. Lank, W. S. Boyd, and F. Cooke. 2002. "A Comparison of the Characteristics and Fate of Barrow's Goldeneye and Bufflehead Nests in Nest Boxes and Natural Cavities." *Condor* 104 (3): 610–619.

Fisher, A. K. 1901. "Two Vanishing Game Birds: The Woodcock and the Wood Duck." In *Yearbook of the United States Department of Agriculture for 1901,* 447–458. Washington, D.C.: Government Printing Office.

Folk, T. H., and G. R. Hepp. 2003. "Effects of Habitat Use and Movement Patterns on Incubation Behavior of Female Wood Ducks (*Aix sponsa*) in Southeast Alabama." *Auk* 120 (4): 1159–1167.

Forbes, P. 2009. *Dazzled and Deceived: Mimicry and Camouflage.* New Haven: Yale University Press.

Forbush, E. H. 1912. *A History of the Game Birds, Wild-Fowl, and Shore Birds of Massachusetts and Adjacent States.* Boston: Wright and Potter Printing Company.

Forbush, E. H. 1925. *Birds of Massachusetts and Other New England States.* Boston: Commonwealth of Massachusetts.

Frank, C. W., Jr. 1982. *Anatomy of a Waterfowl for Carvers and Painters.* Gretna, LA: Pelican.

Frank, W. J. 1948. "Wood Duck Nesting Box Usage in Connecticut." *Journal of Wildlife Management* 12 (2): 128–136.

Fredrickson, L. H. 1988. "Wood Duck Behavior: Fall Courtship to Egg-laying." In *The 1988 North American Wood Duck Symposium,* edited by Leigh H. Fredrickson et al., 35–44. Selected papers from the symposium held in St. Louis, Missouri, February 20–22.

Fredrickson, L. H., and J. L. Hansen. 1983. "Second Broods in Wood Ducks." *Journal of Wildlife Management* 47 (2): 320–326.

Fredrickson, L. H., and S. P. Havera. 2005. "In Memoriam: Frank C. Bellrose, 1916–2005." *Auk* 122: 1298–1300.

Fuller, J. C. 1975. *North Carolina Wood Ducks.* Raleigh: North Carolina Wildlife Resources Commission.

Gallagher, T. 2005. *The Grail Bird: Hot on the Trail of the Ivory-Billed Woodpecker*. Boston: Houghton, Mifflin.

Gauthier, G. 1988. "Factors Affecting Nest-box Use by Buffleheads and Other Cavity-nesting Birds." *Wildlife Society Bulletin* 16 (2): 132–141.

Gigstead, G. 1938. "Wood Ducks in the Illinois River Bottoms." In *Transactions of the Third North American Wildlife Conference*, 603–609. Washington, D.C.: American Wildlife Institute. Papers from the symposium held in Baltimore, Maryland, February 14–17.

Gilmer, D. S., I. J. Ball, L. M. Cowardin, J. E. Mathisen, and J. H. Riechmann. 1978. "Natural Cavities Used by Wood Ducks in North-central Minnesota." *Journal of Wildlife Management* 42 (2): 288–298.

Gilmer, D. S., R. E. Kirby, I. J. Ball, and J. H. Riechmann. 1977. "Post-breeding Activities of Mallards and Wood Ducks in North-central Minnesota." *Journal of Wildlife Management* 41 (3): 345–359.

Goss, N. S. 1891. *History of the Birds of Kansas*. Topeka: Geo. W. Crane.

Gould, S. J. 1992. *Bully for Brontosaurus: Reflections in Natural History*. New York: W. W. Norton.

Granfors, D. A., and L. D. Flake. 1999. "Wood Duck Brood Movements and Habitat Use on Prairie Rivers in South Dakota." *Journal of Wildlife Management* 63 (2): 639–649.

Grice, D., and J. P. Rogers. 1965. *The Wood Duck in Massachusetts*. Final Report: Federal Aid in Wildlife Restoration. Project No. w-19-r. Boston: Massachusetts Division of Fisheries and Game.

Grinnell, G. B. 1901. *American Duck Shooting*. New York: Field and Stream Publishing.

Grinnell, G. B. 1918. *The Game Birds of California*. Self-published.

Hall, V. M. 1961. "Observations of Wood Duck Broods . . ." *Passenger Pigeon* 23 (3): 83–85.

Hamilton, W. D., and M. Zuk. 1982. "Heritable True Fitness and Bright Birds: A Role for Parasites?" *Science* 218: 384–387.

Hanson, H. C. 1951. "Notes on the Artificial Propagation of Wood Duck." *Journal of Wildlife Management* 15c (1): 68–72.

Haramis, G. M. 1988. "Breeding Ecology of the Wood Duck: A Review." In *The 1988 North American Wood Duck Symposium*, edited by Leigh H. Fredrickson et al., 45–60. Selected papers from the symposium held in St. Louis, Missouri, February 20–22.

Haramis, G. M., and D. Q. Thompson. 1984. "Survival of Juvenile Wood Ducks in

Northern Greentree Impoundments." *Journal of Wildlife Management* 48 (4): 1364–1369.

Haramis, G. M., and D. Q. Thompson. 1985. "Density-production Characteristic of Box-nesting Wood Ducks in a Northern Greentree Impoundment." *Journal of Wildlife Management* 49 (2): 429–436.

Hardister, J. P., F. E. Hester, and T. L. Quay. 1962. "Movements of Juvenile Wood Ducks as Measured by Web-tagging." *Proceedings of the Annual Conference of the Southeastern Association of Game and Fish Commissioners* 16: 70–75.

Hartke, K. M., and G. R. Hepp. 2004. "Habitat Use and Preferences of Breeding Female Wood Ducks." *Journal of Wildlife Management* 68 (1): 84–93.

Hartowicz, E. 1965. "Evening Roosting Habits of the Wood Duck in Southeast Missouri." *Journal of Wildlife Management* 29 (2): 399–401.

Hatch, P. L. 1892. *Notes on the Birds of Minnesota*. Minneapolis: Harrison and Smith.

Havera, S. P. 1999. *Waterfowl of Illinois: Status and Management*. Illinois Natural History Survey, Publication 21. Champaign: Illinois Natural History Survey.

Hawkins, A. 1940. "A Wildlife History of Faville Grove, Wisconsin." *Wisconsin Academy of Sciences, Arts, and Letters* 32: 26–65.

Hawkins, A. 1986. "Back Yard Wood Ducks." *Loon* 58 (Winter): 162–166.

Hawkins, A. 1988. "Arthur S. Hawkins 1935." In *Aldo Leopold: Mentor, by His Graduate Students*, edited by R. E. McCabe, 36–45. Madison, WI: Department of Wildlife Ecology, University of Wisconsin-Madison. Proceedings of an Aldo Leopold Centennial Symposium, Madison, WI, April 23–24.

Hawkins, A. 1994. "Aldo Leopold's Contributions to Wood Ducks." *Wood Duck Newsgram*, March, 4.

Hawkins, A., and F. C. Bellrose. 1940. "Wood Duck Management in Illinois." In *Transactions of the Fifth North American Wildlife Conference*, 392–395. Washington, D.C.: Wildlife Management Institute.

Hawkins, A., L. R. Bradley, and R. H. Cunningham. 1988. "Producing Urban and Suburban Wood Ducks." In *The 1988 North American Wood Duck Symposium*, edited by Leigh H. Fredrickson et al., 255–258. Selected papers from the symposium held in St. Louis, Missouri, February 20–22.

Hayden, D. C., and K. H. Pollock. 1988. "Analysis of Wood Duck Banding and Recovery Records, 1970–1986." In *The 1988 North American Wood Duck Symposium*, edited by Leigh H. Fredrickson et al., 361–366. Selected papers from the symposium held in St. Louis, Missouri, February 20–22.

Hein, D. 1966. "Float Counts vs Flight Counts as Indices to Abundance of Nesting Wood Ducks." *Journal of Wildlife Management* 30 (1): 13-16.

Henderson, C. 1992. *Woodworking for Wildlife*. Minneapolis: Minnesota Department of Natural Resources.

Hepp, G. R. 2004. "Early Onset of Incubation by Wood Ducks." *Condor* 106 (1): 182-186.

Hepp, G. R., and J. D. Hair. 1977. "Wood Duck Brood Mobility and Utilization of Beaver Pond Habitats." *Proceedings of the Annual Conference of the Southeastern Association of Fish and Wildlife Agencies* 31: 216-225.

Hepp, G. R., and J. E. Hines. 1991. "Factors Affecting Winter Distribution and Migration Distance of Wood Ducks from Southern Breeding Populations." *Condor* 93 (4): 884-891.

Hepp, G. R., R. T. Hoppe, and R. A. Kennamer. 1987. "Population Parameters and Philopatry of Breeding Female Wood Ducks." *Journal of Wildlife Management* 51 (2): 401-404.

Hepp, G. R., and R. A. Kennamer. 1992. "Characteristics and Consequences of Nest-site Fidelity in Wood Ducks." *Auk* 109 (4) 812-818.

Hepp, G. R., R. A. Kennamer, and W. F. Harvey. 1989. "Recruitment and Natal Philopatry of Wood Ducks." *Ecology* 70 (4): 897-903.

Hepp, G. R., D. J. Stangohr, L. A. Baker, and R. A. Kennamer. 1987. "Factors Affecting Variation in the Egg and Duckling Component of Wood Ducks." *Auk* 104 (3): 435-443.

Hester, F. E., and J. Dermid. 1973. *The World of the Wood Duck*. Philadelphia: J. B. Lippincott.

Heusmann, H. W. 1972. "Survival of Wood Duck Broods from Dump Nests." *Journal of Wildlife Management* 36 (2): 620-624.

Heusmann, H. W. 1984. "The Effects of Weather on Local Wood Duck Production." *Journal of Wildlife Management* 48 (2): 573-577.

Heusmann, H. W. 2000. "Production from Wood Duck Nest Boxes as a Proportion of the Harvest in Massachusetts." *Wildlife Society Bulletin* 28 (4): 1046-1049.

Heusmann, H. W., R. Bellville, and R. G. Burrell. 1980. "Further Observation on Nest Dumping by Wood Ducks." *Journal of Wildlife Management* 44 (4): 908-915.

Heusmann, H. W., and J. E. McDonald. 2002. "Distribution of Wood Duck Harvest in the Atlantic and Mississippi Flyways in Relation to Hunting Season Length." *Wildlife Society Bulletin* 30 (3): 666-674.

Hill, G. 1987. "Why I'm Out There." *Field and Stream* 92 (7): 13.

Hoch, G. 2015. *Booming from the Mists of Nowhere: The Story of the Greater Prairie-Chicken.* Iowa City: University of Iowa Press.

Hoch, G. 2019. *Sky Dance of the Woodcock: The Habits and Habitats of a Strange Little Bird.* Iowa City: University of Iowa Press.

Hocutt, G. E., and R. W. Dimmick. 1971. "Summer Food Habits of Juvenile Wood Ducks in East Tennessee." *Journal of Wildlife Management* 35 (2): 286-292.

Hornaday, W. T. 1904. *Hornaday's American Natural History.* New York: Charles Scribner's Sons.

Hornaday, W. T. 1913. *Our Vanishing Wild Life: Its Extermination and Preservation.* New York: New York Zoological Society.

Howell, A. H. 1911. *Birds of Arkansas.* U.S. Department of Agriculture Biological Survey, Bulletin No. 38. Washington, D.C.: U.S. Department of Agriculture.

Howell, S. N. G. 2010. *Molt in North American Birds.* Boston: Houghton Mifflin Harcourt.

Humphrey, P. S., and K. C. Parkes. 1959. "An Approach to the Study of Molts and Plumages." *Auk* 76: 1-31.

Huntington, D. W. 1903. *Our Feathered Game: A Handbook of the North American Game Birds.* New York: Charles Scribner's Sons.

Jackson, J. A. 2004. *In Search of the Ivory-Billed Woodpecker.* Washington, D.C.: Smithsonian Books.

Jackson, J. A. 2007. *George Miksch Sutton: Artist, Scientist, and Teacher.* Norman: University of Oklahoma Press.

Jansen, R. W., and E. K. Bollinger. 1998. "Effects of Nest-box Visibility and Clustering on Wood Duck Brood Parasitism in Illinois." *Transactions of the Illinois Academy of Science* 91 (3-4): 161-166.

Jarosz, J. A. 1960. "Food Habits of the Wood Duck." *Flicker* 32 (June): 61.

Johnsgard, P. A. 1968. *Waterfowl: Their Biology and Natural History.* Lincoln: University of Nebraska Press.

Johnsgard, P. A. 1976. *The Bird Decoy: An American Art Form.* Lincoln: University of Nebraska Press.

Johnsgard, P. A. 2010. "The World's Waterfowl in the 21st Century: A 2010 Supplement to *Ducks, Geese, and Swans of the World.*" http://digitalcommons.unl.edu/biosciducksgeeseswans/20.

Johnston, C. A., and R. J. Naiman. 1990. "Aquatic Patch Creation in Relation to Beaver Population Trends." *Ecology* 71 (4): 1617-1621.

Jones, R. E., and A. S. Leopold. 1967. "Nesting Interference in a Dense Population of Wood Ducks." *Journal of Wildlife Management* 31 (2): 221–228.

Kaminski, R. M., R. W. Alexander, and B. D. Leopold. 1993. "Wood Duck and Mallard Winter Microhabitats in Mississippi Hardwood Bottomlands." *Journal of Wildlife Management* 57 (3): 562–570.

Kaminski, R. M., J. B. Davis, H. W. Essig, P. D. Gerard, and K. J. Reinecke. 2003. "True Metabolizable Energy for Wood Ducks from Acorns Compared to Other Waterfowl Foods." *Journal of Wildlife Management* 67 (3): 542–550.

Kelly, D., and V. L. Sork. 2002. "Mast Seeding in Perennial Plants: Why, How, Where?" *Annual Review of Ecology and Systematics* 33: 427–447.

Kelly, J. R. 1996. "Line-transect Sampling for Estimating Breeding Wood Duck Density in Forested Wetlands." *Wildlife Society Bulletin* 24 (1): 32–36.

Kelly, J. R. 2003. "The Role of Banding in Wood Duck Management." *Wood Duck Newsgram*, November, 1–3.

Kennamer, R. A. 2001. "Relating Climatological Patterns to Wetland Conditions and Wood Duck Production in the Southeastern Atlantic Coastal Plain." *Wildlife Society Bulletin* 29 (4): 1193–1205.

Kennamer, R. A., W. F. Harvey IV, and G. R. Hepp. 1990. "Embryonic Development and Nest Attentiveness of Wood Ducks during Egg Laying." *Condor* 92 (3): 587–592.

Kennamer, R. A., and G. R. Hepp. 1987. "Frequency and Timing of Second Broods in Wood Ducks." *Wilson Bulletin* 99 (4): 655–662.

Kennard, F. H. 1915. "The Okaloacoochee Slough." *Auk* 32 (2): 154–166.

Kerlinger, P. 1995. *How Birds Migrate*. Mechanicsburg, PA: Stackpole Books.

Kilgo, J. 1988. *Deep Enough for Ivorybills: A Memorable Look at Hunting, Fishing—and Companionship—in the South*. New York: Doubleday.

King, W. R. 1866. *Naturalist in Canada, Or Notes on the Natural History of the Game, Game Birds, and Fish of That Country*. London: Hurst and Blackett.

Knight, O. W. 1908. *The Birds of Maine*. Bangor, ME: published by the author.

Koenig, W. D., J. M. H. Knops, W. J. Carmen, and I. S. Pearse. 2015. "What Drives Masting? The Phenological Synchrony Hypothesis." *Ecology* 96 (1): 184–192.

Korschgen, C. E., and L. H. Fredrickson. 1976. "Comparative Displays of Yearling and Adult Male Wood Ducks." *Auk* 93 (4): 793–807.

Kortright, F. H. 1943. *The Ducks, Geese, and Swans of North America*. Washington, D.C.: American Wildlife Institute.

Krohne, D. 2008. "River Blindness." *Wabash College Magazine*, Fall, 87–89.

Kumlien, L., and N. Hollister. 1903. *The Bird of Wisconsin.* Reprinted, Madison: Wisconsin Society for Ornithology, 1951.

LeMaster, E. T., and R. E. Trost. 1994. "Summer Survival Rate Estimates of Adult Wood Ducks: Implications for Banding Programs." *Journal of Wildlife Management* 58 (1): 107–114.

LeMaster, R. 1985. *The Great Gallery of Ducks and Other Waterfowl.* Mechanicsburg, PA: Stackpole Books.

Leopold, A. 1933. *Game Management.* New York: Charles Scribner's Sons.

Leopold, A. 1942. "The Role of Wildlife in a Liberal Education." In *Transactions of the Seventh North American Wildlife Conference,* 485–489. Washington, D.C.: American Wildlife Institute.

Leopold, A. 1949. *A Sand County Almanac.* New York: Oxford University Press.

Leopold, A. 1999. *For the Health of the Land: Previously Unpublished Essays and Other Writings.* Edited by J. B. Callicott and E. T. Freyfogle. Washington, D.C.: Island Press.

Leopold, A. 2013. *Leopold: A Sand County Almanac and Other Writings on Ecology and Conservation.* Edited by C. Meine. New York: Library of America.

Leopold, F. 1951. "A Study of Nesting Wood Ducks in Iowa." *Condor* 53 (5): 209–220.

Leopold, F. 1953. "Wood Duck Nesting Records, Volume 1, 1939–1953." Frederic Leopold Papers, MS 113, Iowa State University Library Special Collections and University Archives.

Leopold, F. 1966. "Experience with Home-grown Wood Ducks." In *Wood Duck Management and Ecology: A Symposium,* 113–123. Washington, D.C.: Office of Biological Services, U.S. Fish and Wildlife Service.

Leopold, F. 1984. "A Duck Hunter." In *Flyways: Pioneering Waterfowl Management in North America,* edited by A. S. Hawkins, R. C. Hanson, H. K. Nelson, and H. M. Reeves, 20–26. Washington, D.C.: U.S. Fish and Wildlife Service.

Lewis, E. J. 1906. *The American Sportsman.* Philadelphia: J. B. Lippincott.

Lincoln, F. C. 1921. "The History and Purpose of Bird Banding." *Auk* 38 (2): 217–228.

Livezey, B. C. 1986. "A Phylogenetic Analysis of Recent Anseriform Genera Using Morphological Characters." *Auk* 103 (4): 737–754.

Longley, B. 1993. "Competitors for Wood Duck Boxes." *Wood Duck Newsgram,* December, 6.

Lowney, M. S., and E. P. Hill. 1989. "Wood Duck Nest Sites in Bottomland Hardwood Forests of Mississippi." *Journal of Wildlife Management* 53 (2): 378–382.

Luce, D. 2003. "In Memoriam: Walter Breckenridge." *Minnesota Conservation Volunteer*, September-October, 62-63.

Maass, D. 1990. *The Wildfowl Art of David Maass*. Camden: Briar Patch.

Mabbott, D. C. 1920. *Food Habits of Seven Species of American Shoal-Water Ducks*. U.S. Department of Agriculture, Bulletin No. 862. Washington, D.C.: U.S. Department of Agriculture.

Mackey, W. J. 1965. *American Bird Decoys*. New York: E.P. Dutton.

Madson, J. 1985. *Up on the River: With People and Wildlife of the Upper Mississippi*. New York: Lyons.

Mallory, M. L., A. Taverner, B. Bower, and D. Crook. 2002. "Wood Duck and Hooded Merganser Breeding Success in Nest Boxes in Ontario." *Wildlife Society Bulletin* 30 (2): 310-316.

Manlove, C. A., and G. R. Hepp. 2000. "Patterns of Nest Attendance in Female Wood Ducks." *Condor* 102 (2): 286-291.

Martin, E. M., and A. O. Haugen. 1960. "Seasonal Changes in Wood Duck Roosting Flight Habits." *Wilson Bulletin* 72 (3): 238-243.

Martin, T. E., and P. Li. "Life History of Open- vs. Cavity-nesting Birds." *Ecology* 73 (2): 579-592.

Maynard, C. J. 1916. *A Field Ornithology of the Birds of Eastern North America*. Copyright C. J. Maynard. Published by author.

McAtee, W. L. 1939. *Wildfowl Food Plants: Their Value, Propagation, and Management*. Ames: Collegiate Press.

McCabe, R. A. 1947. "The Homing of Transplanted Wood Ducks." *Wilson Bulletin* 59 (2): 104-109.

McComb, W. C., and R. E. Noble. 1981. "Nest-box and Natural-cavity Use in Three Mid-South Forest Habitats." *Journal of Wildlife Management* 45 (1): 93-101.

McGilvrey, F. B. 1966. "Fall Food Habits of Wood Ducks from Lake Marion, South Carolina." *Journal of Wildlife Management* 30 (1): 193-195.

McGilvrey, F. B. 1969. "Survival in Wood Duck Broods." *Journal of Wildlife Management* 33 (1): 73-76.

McLaughlin, C. L., and D. Grice. 1952. "Effectiveness of Large-scale Erection of Wood Duck Boxes as a Management Procedure." In *Transactions of the Seventeenth North American Wildlife and Natural Resources Conference*, 242-259. Washington, D.C.: Wildlife Management Institute.

McQueeny, E. M. 1946. *Prairie Wings, Pen and Camera Flight Studies*. Exton, PA: Schiffer.

McQuilken, R. A., and R. A. Musbach. 1977. "Pin Oak Acorn Production on Green Tree Reservoirs in Southeastern Missouri." *Journal of Wildlife Management* 41 (2): 218–225.

McRobbie, L. R. 2016. "When the British Wanted to Camouflage Their Warships, They Made Them Dazzle." https://www.smithsonianmag.com/history/when-british -wanted-camouflage-their-warships-they-made-them-dazzle-180958657/.

Morse, T. E., and H. M. Wight. 1969. "Dump Nesting and Its Effects on Production in Wood Ducks." *Journal of Wildlife Management* 33 (2): 284–293.

Musselman, T. E. 1948. "A Changing Nesting Habitat of the Wood Duck." *Auk* 65 (2): 197–203.

Nelson, C. H. 1993. *The Downy Waterfowl of North America.* Deerfield: Delta Station.

Nelson, H. K. 1988. "Development of a Suburban Wood Duck Nesting Colony in Bloomington, Minnesota." *Loon* 60 (Spring): 34–36.

Nelson, H. K. 2001. "A Suburban Wood Duck Patch: 20 Year History." *Wood Duck Newsgram*, July, 1–5.

Nelson, H. K., J. R. Serie, and D. L. Trauger. 2007. "Arthur S. Hawkins." *Journal of Wildlife Management* 71 (1): 297–298.

Nichols, C. K. 1937. "Early Nesting of the Wood Duck." *Auk* 54 (4): 533.

Oates, D. W., and J. D. Principato. 1994. "Genetic Variation and Differentiation of North American Waterfowl (Anatidae)." *Transactions of the Nebraska Academy of Sciences* 21: 127–145.

Parr, D. E., M. D. Scott, and D. D. Kennedy. 1979. "Autumn Movements and Habitat Use by Wood Ducks in Southern Illinois." *Journal of Wildlife Management* 43 (1): 102–108.

Petrie, C. 1987. "Reflections on a Wood Duck Pond." In *Autumn Passages: A Ducks Unlimited Treasury of Waterfowling Classics.* Minocqua, WI: Willow Creek.

Phillips, J. C. 1925. *A Natural History of the Ducks. Vols. III and IV.* Cambridge: Riverside.

Porter, G. S. 1919. *Homing with the Birds; The History of a Lifetime of Personal Experience with the Birds.* New York: Doubleday, Page.

Prince, H. H. 1968. "Nest Sites Used by Wood Ducks and Common Goldeneye in New Brunswick." *Journal of Wildlife Management* 32 (3): 489–500.

Pyle, P. 2005. "Molts and Plumages of Ducks (Anatinae)." *Waterbirds* 28 (2): 208–219.

Pyle, P. 2008. *Identification Guide to North American Birds. Part II.* Point Reyes, CA: Slate Creek.

Rankin, N. 2008. *"A Genius for Deception": How Cunning Helped the British Win Two World Wars*. New York: Oxford University Press.

Ransom, D., and C. D. Frentress. 2007. "Monitoring Texas Wood Ducks with a Cooperative Nest Box Program." *Journal of Wildlife Management* 71 (8): 2743-2748.

Ransom, D., R. L. Honeycutt, and R. D. Slack. 2001. "Population Genetics of Southeastern Wood Ducks." *Journal of Wildlife Management* 65 (4): 746-754.

Reed, C. A. 1912. *Birds of Eastern North America*. New York: Doubleday, Page.

Reed, C. A. 1936. *Bird Guide: Water Birds, Game Birds and Birds of Prey East of the Rockies*. Garden City: Doubleday, Doran.

Reeves, H. M. 1988. "The Wood Duck: Some Historical and Cultural Aspects." In *The 1988 North American Wood Duck Symposium*, edited by Leigh H. Fredrickson et al., 3-12. Selected papers from the symposium held in St. Louis, Missouri, February 20-22.

Reiger, G. 1994. *Heron Hills Chronicle*. New York: Lyons and Burfords.

Reiger, G. 2000. *A Complete Book of North American Waterfowling*. New York: Lyons.

Renouf, R. N. 1972. "Waterfowl Utilization of Beaver Ponds in New Brunswick." *Journal of Wildlife Management* 36 (3): 740-744.

Ridgway, R. 1913. *The Ornithology of Illinois. Volume II*. Springfield: Published by the authority of the State Legislature.

Ripley, D. 1957. *A Paddling of Ducks*. New York: Harcourt, Brace.

Robb, J. R., and T. A. Bookout. 1995. "Factors Influencing Wood Duck Use of Natural Cavities." *Journal of Wildlife Management* 59 (2): 372-383.

Roberts, T. S. 1932. *The Birds of Minnesota*. Minneapolis: University of Minnesota Press.

Rondeau, T. 2007. "Wood Duck Band Recoveries." *Wood Duck Newsgram*, November, 10.

Ronning, N. 2011. "Agassiz National Wildlife Refuge: Minnesota's Bufflehead Factory." *Wood Duck Newsgram*, November, 4-5.

Roosevelt, T. 1911. "Revealing and Concealing Coloration in Birds and Mammals." *Bulletin of the American Museum of Natural History* 30: 119-231.

Rowher, F. C., and H. W. Heusmann. 1991. "Effects of Brood Size and Age on Survival of Female Wood Ducks." *Condor* 93 (4): 817-824.

Roy Nielsen, C. L., R. J. Gates, and P. G. Parker. 2006. "Intraspecific Nest Parasitism of Wood Ducks in Natural Cavities: Comparisons with Nest Boxes." *Journal of Wildlife Management* 70 (3): 835-843.

Roy Nielsen, C. L., and R.J. Gates. 2007. "Reduced Nest Predation of Cavity-nesting

Wood Ducks during Flooding in a Bottomland Hardwood Forest." *Condor* 109 (1): 210–215.

Roy Nielsen, C. L., R. J. Gates, and E. H. Zwicker. 2007. "Projected Availability of Natural Cavities for Wood Ducks in Southern Illinois." *Journal of Wildlife Management* 71 (3): 875–883.

Ryan, D. C., R. J. Kawula, and R. J. Gates. 1998. "Breeding Biology of Wood Ducks Using Natural Cavities in Southern Illinois." *Journal of Wildlife Management* 62 (1): 112–123.

Sandys, E. 1905. "Sporting Sketches." Quoted in S. Miller, *Early American Waterfowling 1700s–1930*. Piscataway, NJ: New Century, 1986.

Savard, J-P. L. and M. Robert. 2007. "Use of Nest Boxes by Goldeneyes in Eastern North America." *Wilson Journal of Ornithology* 119 (1): 28–34.

Semel, B., and P. W. Sherman. 1986. "Dynamics of Nest Parasitism in Wood Ducks." *Auk* 103 (4): 813–816.

Semel, B., and P. W. Sherman. 1992. "Use of Clutch Size to Infer Brood Parasitism in Wood Ducks." *Journal of Wildlife Management* 56 (3): 495–499.

Semel, B., and P. W. Sherman. 1995. "Alternative Placement Strategies for Wood Duck Nest Boxes." *Wildlife Society Bulletin* 23 (3): 463–471.

Semel, B., P. W. Sherman, and S. M. Byers. 1988. "Effects of Brood Parasitism and Nest-box Placement on Wood Duck Breeding Ecology." *Condor* 90 (4): 920–930.

Seton, E. T. 1929. *Lives of Game Animals: Volume IV – Part II*. New York: Doubleday, Doran.

Sherman, D. E., R. M. Kaminski, and B. D. Leopold. 1992. "Potential Indices of Mallard and Wood Duck Abundance in Forested Wetlands during Winter." *Wildlife Society Bulletin* 20 (2): 148–156.

Shurtleff, L. L., and C. Savage. 1996. *The Wood Duck and the Mandarin*. Berkeley: University of California Press.

Sibley, D. A., C. Elphick, and J. B. Dunning, Jr. 2001. *The Sibley Guide to Bird Life and Behavior*. New York: Chanticleer Press.

Sincock, J. L., M. M. Smith, and J. J. Lynch. 1964. "Ducks in Dixie." In *Waterfowl Tomorrow*, edited by J. P. Linduska, 99–108. Washington, D.C.: U.S. Fish and Wildlife Service.

Smith, R. L., and L. D. Flake. 1985. "Movements and Habitats of Brood-rearing Wood Ducks on a Prairie River." *Journal of Wildlife Management* 49 (2): 437–442.

Soulliere, G. J. 1986. "Cost and Significance of a Wood Duck Nest-house Program in Wisconsin: An Evaluation." *Wildlife Society Bulletin* 14 (4): 391–395.

Soulliere, G. J. 1988. "Density of Suitable Wood Duck Nest Cavities in a Northern Hardwood Forest." *Journal of Wildlife Management* 52 (1): 86–89.

Soulliere, G. J., M. A. Al-Saffar, J. M. Coluccy, R. J. Gates, H. M. Hagy, J. W. Simpson, J. N. Straub, R. L. Pierce, M. W. Eichholz, and D. R. Luukkonen. 2017. *Upper Mississippi River and Great Lakes Region Joint Venture Waterfowl Habitat Conservation Strategy—2017 Revision.* Bloomington, MN: U.S. Fish and Wildlife Service.

Stephens, S. E., R. M. Kaminski, B. D. Leopold, and P. D. Gerard. 1998. "Reproduction of Wood Ducks in Large and Small Nest Boxes." *Wildlife Society Bulletin* 26 (1): 159–167.

Stewart, P. A. 1958. "Locomotion in Wood Ducks." *Wilson Bulletin* 70 (2): 184–187.

Straka, S. 2012. "Wood Duck Reflections and Tales." *Wood Duck Newsgram*, March, 6.

Strand, R. 2000. "Monitoring Wood Ducks." *Wood Duck Newsgram*, July, 3, 11.

Strand, R. 2001. "Candid Camera." *Wood Duck Newsgram*, April, 4–5.

Strand, R. 2002. "Wood Duck Nest Boxes, a Late Summer Trap Line." *Wood Duck Newsgram*, July, 6–7.

Strand, R. 2005. "Counting the Hatch." *Wood Duck Newsgram*, November, 10–11.

Strand, R. 2006. "Goldeneyes." *Wood Duck Newsgram*, November, 6–7.

Strand, R. 2007. "Counting the Hatch, Updated." *Wood Duck Newsgram*, July, 6–7.

Strand, R. 2014. "High Definition Hens." *Wood Duck Newsgram*, July, 18.

Strange, T. H., E. R. Cunningham, and J. W. Goertz. 1971. "Use of Nest Boxes by Wood Ducks in Mississippi." *Journal of Wildlife Management* 35 (4): 786–793.

Sutton, G. M. 1979. *To a Young Bird Artist: Letters from Louis Agassiz Fuertes to George Miksch Sutton.* Norman: University of Oklahoma Press.

Tanner, J. T. 1942. *The Ivory-Billed Woodpecker.* Research Report Number 1. New York: National Audubon Society.

Thaxter, C. 1886. "Women's Heartlessness." http://www.seacoastnh.com/celia-thaxter-attacks-heartless-women-wearing-birds-as-fashion/.

Thayer, G. H. 1909. *Concealing-coloration in the Animal Kingdom.* New York: Trow.

Thomforde, L. 2014. "Banding Wood Ducks on Arnold's Farm." *Wood Duck Newsgram*, July, 7.

Thompson, J. D., and G. A. Baldassarre. 1989. "Postbreeding Dispersal by Wood Ducks in Northern Alabama with Reference to Early Hunting Seasons." *Wildlife Society Bulletin* 17 (2): 142–146.

Thoreau, H. D. 1855. *The Journals of Henry David Thoreau: Volume 8.* Reprinted, Sportsman's Vintage Press, 2016.

Tordoff, H. B. 2004. "In Memoriam: Walter John Breckenridge, 1903–2003." *Auk* 121 (4): 1286–1288.

Townsend, C. W. 1916. "The Courtship of the Merganser, Mallard, Black Duck, Baldpate, Wood Duck, and Bufflehead." *Auk* 33 (1): 9–17.

Utsey, F. M., and G. R. Hepp. 1997. "Frequency of Nest Box Maintenance: Effects on Wood Duck Nesting in South Carolina." *Journal of Wildlife Management* 61 (3): 801–807.

Yetter, A. P., S. P. Havera, and C. S. Hines. 1999. "Natural-cavity Use by Nesting Wood Ducks in Illinois." *Journal of Wildlife Management* 63 (2): 630–638.

Yorke, F. H. 1899. *Our Ducks: A History of American Ducks, Nesting, Roosting, Feeding, and Playing Grounds: Habits Throughout the Year.* Chicago: American Field.

Webster, C. G., and F. B. McGilvrey. 1966. "Providing Brood Habitat for Wood Ducks." In *Wood Duck Management and Research: A Symposium*, 70–74. Washington, D.C.: Office of Biological Services, U.S. Fish and Wildlife Service.

Weier, R. W. 1966. "Survey of Wood Duck Nest Sites on Mingo National Wildlife Refuge." In *Wood Duck Management and Research: A Symposium*, 91–107. Washington, D.C.: Office of Biological Services, U.S. Fish and Wildlife Service.

Wilson, A. 1839. *Wilson's American Ornithology, with Notes from Jardine.* New York: T. L. Magagnos.

Wolfe, T. 1989. "A Tribute to 946-98303." *Wood Duck Newsgram*, September, 7.

Wood, H. B. 1945. "The History of Bird Banding." *Auk* 62 (2): 256–265.

Wood Duck Management and Research: A Symposium. 1966. http://wildlife.org/wp-content/uploads/2015/12/Jahn_etal_1966-WODUManagement_300dpi.pdf.

Zicus, M. C., and S. K. Hennes. 1987. "Use of Nest Boxes to Monitor Cavity-nesting Waterfowl Populations." *Wildlife Society Bulletin* 15 (4): 525–532.

Zicus, M. C., and S. K. Hennes. 1989. "Nest Prospecting by Common Goldeneyes." *Condor* 91 (4): 807–812.

Zimmerman, G. S., J. R. Sauer, K. Fleming, W. A. Link, and P. R. Garrettson. 2015. "Combining Waterfowl and Breeding Bird Survey Data to Estimate Wood Duck Breeding Population Size in the Atlantic Flyway." *Journal of Wildlife Management* 79 (7): 1051–1061.

index

The Tallgrass Prairie Center Guide to Prairie Restoration in the Upper Midwest
By Daryl Smith, Dave Williams, Greg Houseal, and Kirk Henderson

Up on the River: People and Wildlife of the Upper Mississippi
By John Madson

Where the Sky Began: Land of the Tallgrass Prairie
By John Madson

Wildflowers and Other Plants of Iowa Wetlands
By Sylvan Runkel and Dean Roosa

Wildflowers of Iowa Woodlands
By Sylvan Runkel and Alvin Bull

Wildflowers of the Tallgrass Prairie: The Upper Midwest
By Sylvan Runkel and Dean Roosa

With Wings Extended: A Leap into the Wood Duck's World
By Greg Hoch

Made in the USA
Monee, IL
08 April 2021

65198147R00112